For Henry Beston
with warm regards -

Van Wyck Brooks

September: 1961

See page 19 - 20 - 21

FROM THE SHADOW OF THE MOUNTAIN

VAN WYCK BROOKS *has written:*

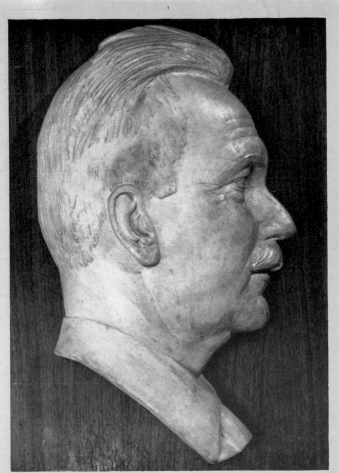

VAN WYCK BROOKS
Bas-relief in terra cotta, 1943
by Paul Manship

FROM THE SHADOW
OF THE MOUNTAIN

My Post-Meridian Years

By Van Wyck Brooks

E. P. DUTTON & COMPANY, INC.
NEW YORK, 1961

Published simultaneously in Canada
by Clarke, Irwin & Co., Ltd., of Toronto

Library of Congress Catalog Card Number: 61-11417

PRINTED IN THE UNITED STATES OF AMERICA
AMERICAN BOOK–STRATFORD PRESS, INC., NEW YORK

NOTE

THIS IS THE THIRD AND FINAL VOLUME of a series
that relates the story of my life. It follows *Scenes
and Portraits: Memories of Childhood and Youth*
and *Days of the Phoenix: The Nineteen-Twenties
I Remember.*

CONTENTS

FROM THE SHADOW OF THE MOUNTAIN

CHAPTER I

AT WESTPORT

WHEN I emerged, in 1931, from the shadow of the mountain,—to use an old expression of the Hudson river,— I felt, after four years passed in mental hospitals, decidedly young again but rather dazed. I did not quite feel like the Prisoner of Chillon who "regained his freedom with a sigh," but there remained in my stomach as it were a hard ball of panic that was never entirely to disappear. It was a glorious May afternoon and I remember the sunlight falling on rugs and pictures through the western windows of our little white cottage in the village of Westport, but this light was somehow strange and, even when I had recovered my balance, this strangeness was to linger in the air. I knew that every decade now was supposed to bring in a different world, that the thirties were to differ from the twenties as, in time, the forties were to differ from the thirties and so on; but a kind of murky mental weather had set in with the thirties that was unlike the clarity of the decade before. The new world seemed to be all a Magic Mountain like the International Sanitorium Berghof of Thomas Mann's novel. There Joaquin said to Hans Castorf, "The climate isn't the only queer thing about us. You're going to see some things you've never dreamed of. Just wait."

The sibyl Gertrude Stein spoke of this change of atmosphere. One could no longer, she said, be realistic when things had ceased to be real and become strange; and H. G. Wells also referred to the "frightful queerness" that had come into modern life. In fact, in the ocean of relativity that was all about us now, fixed points on the shore had largely vanished. Everybody spoke of the uncertainty of values in this "age of anxiety," as it came to be called, or this "sexual era," as others described a time that was marked by Lee Simonson's "visas over the sexual border." The familiar notions of time, space and natural law, and even of human personality, had faded out. Artists and writers were impelled to express a social consciousness, it is true, that stood for a surviving reality, the idea of justice; and this was the time of the League of American Writers when Hemingway spoke at a congress in Carnegie Hall. I cannot forget the excitement when he appeared on the platform before he went off to Cuba and became a legend. These, moreover, were the years when John Dos Passos produced his bitter trilogy *U.S.A.* But, in the "proletarian thirties," among the young men who surrounded us, who had often sat on the terrace outside the Dome, or who had been sitting in the Ritz bar in Paris when the stock market at home suddenly crashed, among these young men ideas that were strange in the light of all that had gone before, spoke of the new dehumanization of art. As if the problems of life and the world had become too difficult to face, an art was gradually appearing that was really a game, based on a "loathing for the human," as Ortega put it; and at the same time one heard of the "power of blackness," in Melville's phrase, that was utterly routing the traditional power of light. These notes became more pronounced as time went on.

One suddenly heard, on every side, the solemn word "security," expressing the one felt want of the new generation, security at almost any price for young men who, in the first world war, had suffered as many risks as they could take. The old desire of youth for adventure, in the outward sense at least, seemed to have been snuffed out in this greatest of adventures, and, where everything appeared unreal and strange, one could understand the general wish for a life in which one took no chances. There were misgivings everywhere in this time of troubles, and one found offered for sale even on drugstore counters Kierkegaard's *Fear and Trembling* and *Sickness unto Death*. It was the time when Willa Cather rose to fame because of the calm, the repose that marked her stories, because of her love for the reassuring solidity and depth of old adobe walls and granite dwellings. Meanwhile, to return to the Magic Mountain, its cosmopolitan population, with Russians, Danes and Italians gathered together, Bulgarians, Poles, Mexicans and what not, also marked our little Westport where a new feeling for the planet as a whole had spread as another result of the first world war. This was different indeed from the world-mindedness of the nineteenth century that seemed in the twentieth so provincial, the state of mind of Saint-Simon, for instance, in whose ideal society there were to be four governmental divisions. The whole of Asia and Africa were to be under the jurisdiction of England, Italy, Germany and France, and what Occidental did not think this entirely just? But John Gunther had settled in Westport where Vincent Sheean came for a while to live in an old house across the street, types of the new correspondent who had been behind the scenes in Europe, in Russia, in Asia, everywhere. These men seemed almost to have been born with a pluralistic view of mankind. Nothing less provincial could have been imagined.

Vincent Sheean symbolized, for me, the Middle West, the provenance then of so much of our art and letters, where Frank

Lloyd Wright and Hemingway had grown up near Chicago and where so many, like Sandburg, were now living. Sheean was a product of what Sherwood Anderson called the "Robin's egg Renaissance" before the robin's egg dropped out of the nest. Virtually a man of the world from birth, he had plunged, almost as a boy, into the turmoil of Europe in the early twenties, easily picking up languages and prepared, as he wrote, to "deal with the largest doings of the great." He was thrown with all the statesmen whose measure he took in his *Personal History,* and what Robinson Jeffers called the "dull welter of Asia" was, for Sheean, putting forth new shoots of life. He was to write before long his book on Gandhi, and, having known Primo de Rivera in Spain, he could not believe that H. G. Wells had said a good word for the autocratic Franco. This must have been later in the thirties, during the Spanish civil war, and I had met, in New York, at dinner, this novelist who had once called Franco the "murderous little Christian gentleman." Yet, as opposed to the Loyalists, Wells supported Franco now, saying that he was going to establish a liberal monarchy and the English knew how to deal with men like that. He grew even more emphatic when Franz Werfel, who was present, expostulated, "But Mr. Wells! But Mr. Wells!" Vincent Sheean, who had played tennis with Wells on the Riviera, could not believe anything so uncharacteristic.

But Sheean, with his world-consciousness, would have liked the plan that Wells expounded for a world-encyclopædia. Wells had found Harvard congenial, saying of President Conant, "He's a great fellow, he agreed with every word I said"; but he was much concerned that evening with the decline of his own vogue to which he referred vaguely two or three times. He said, "American criticism has always floated on a magic island," which seemed to me, with the "new" critics, truer than ever;

and he remarked at dinner, "At that time I was seeing much of a great American novelist, the man who started all modern writing. Now I wonder who knows the man I mean?" He looked around blankly and nobody answered until I said, "Stephen Crane," whereupon he gave me a hearty handshake. At ten o'clock, taking out his watch, he said he had to go home; then, instantly, he sat down and talked till midnight about the encyclopædia he had in mind. He said a new dark age was coming and the only hope was to assemble all knowledge in the manner of Diderot and his circle. This could be kept underground till the next renaissance.

Although he was seventy-two years old, Wells had not yet reached the final despair in which he wrote *Mind at the End of Its Tether,* saying, "The end of everything we call life is close at hand" and our world of self-delusion is destined to perish. He seemed to have reversed the point of view with which, as a novelist, he had been preëminently a story-teller; and in fact the story was fading away from the novel now,—the story was turned over to the writers of whodunits. The new novelists generally agreed with Sartre about "the foolish business of mere story-telling." Nor was this the only respect in which the fiction of the future was to differ from the fiction of the twenties and earlier years. Theodore Dreiser, like Sinclair Lewis or Ellen Glasgow or Willa Cather, reflected to a large extent the communal life; they presented a broad picture of the society of their time while they created characters that stood for it. Their novels were the products of "saturation," the word that Henry James used for an intimate understanding of the social scene, obtained either by birth or study, but in any case essential and the real *terra firma* of a novelist's art. I wondered how far the world-consciousness that I saw all about me was destined to preclude this saturation, this giving of oneself to a definite locale to the close knowledge of which novelists had once devoted so much attention. The young men I knew were more often familiar with Munich or Paris or Mexico City than with their own Denver or Omaha or Trenton, and this left them with no deep attachment to the country of their origin, still less to any more restricted region. There could be no saturation with any human society in a world that "annihilated distance," as Toynbee put it; and the result was to be what Malcolm Cowley presently described in his book *The Literary Situation*. Every novel came to be dismissed as "naturalistic" that gave a broad picture of a social scene, and "the only novel recognized as worthy" was "one that presents at most a crisis in the lives of a few individuals." Moreover, the study of form without regard to content left some of the novelists high and dry, with no society behind them to write about and with only exotic characters and marginal themes.

In Westport we were surrounded with world-conscious minds like Hendrik van Loon, the historical story-teller, the lover of wit and music, good food, good wine, tolerance and all the other Erasmian virtues. In Hendrik's alphabet, B for Borobadour followed A for Athens, and he included Oahu with London and Rome. His *Story of Mankind* created for children the kind of expanded point of view they derived from Nehru's *Glimpses of World History,* in which Siam and Belgium, Sweden and Afghanistan appeared side by side in all their phases. Hendrik was more and more obsessed with the second world war that was coming and that was to destroy in time his beloved Middelburg, the old abbey and all his childhood recollections. Meanwhile, the old-fashioned well-trained English novelist, William McFee, still lived in Westport, though he had "no roots anywhere," he said, "save in the fenceless meadows of the sea . . . No background, only a series of backdrops." He had been born on a ship with sea-faring parents who had moved from Canada to London; and, spending his life among Arabs and Greeks, Russians and Chinese, he had remained indefeasibly English. Yet after 1908 he had never lived in England, where he had written his first novel. As a sea-going engineer, writing on watches or in port, he had roamed from Smyrna to Constantinople, from Port Said to Salonica, from the Danube to the Amazon, spending his nights ashore in the wineshops of the world. To the steady drum of the engines, he had listened to the passengers, like his own Mr. Spenlove, the engineer, and his astonishment never ceased at the ways of the Americans and their effect on English men and women. He moved up to Brookfield, eventually, where the country recalled the Malvern Hills,—"These hills will always be my love," he wrote; and then again he moved to a lonely road in Roxbury where he stowed himself away in a tiny cottage. With a ship's bell outside, it was as snug as the captain's cabin in a well-built tramp on the Indian ocean; and there, while he freely aired his prejudices, he read almost every novel that came out. He remarked that American fiction was in the same stage as the drama in Elizabethan times when it was all melodrama; and, calling himself a troglodite, he said he was one of the last of the story-tellers.

In fact, modern writing, as it was called from this time on, was largely the creation of displaced persons, T. S. Eliot and Ezra Pound, James Joyce and Gertrude Stein, all of whom had left behind the countries of their origin and for whom human beings were more or less abstractions. Seceding from what was called mass-culture, they had lost touch with the common humanity that had moved the novelists of the twenties; and yet there was no returning to the concrete world they had left behind or any escape from the planetary feeling of the present.

"Isn't the end of literature somehow already in sight?" a sensitive Austrian émigré wrote to me, and others were writing essays on the "death of poetry" or on the "death of the novel." One of my friends wrote to me, "Since last I saw you the turn of events has more and more convinced me that literature, *per se,* belongs to a time and a cultural atmosphere that no longer exists. So I turn to politics," he continued; but even if it meant the possible death of literature, one could scarcely regret a tendency that brought the world together. Actually, in the atomic age, a world-wide social unity was necessary for everyone's existence, and how could one oppose the kind of world-brotherhood which the mixture of races in America was bringing about? Many of my friends shared this planetary feeling, whether George Biddle or Jo Davidson or Thornton Wilder or Glenway Wescott, who had said *Good-bye to Wisconsin* and had never found another world that he was able to reconstruct in fiction, although in *The Pilgrim Hawk* and *Apartment in Athens* he had written fine isolated studies of foreign settings. Novels, sporadic novels, might continue to be written; but, without saturation, with no immersion in a social scene, could there be novelists of the old massive kind?

There was Sherwood Anderson, never by nature a novelist, although he had experienced the saturation that marked him as a man of the pre-war time; and it was this that gave his best short stories the note of authenticity of one who has "been there." As for literary influences, the odd characters of George Borrow had reminded him of his own small-town people and helped him in a way to shape them in his work; and, just as Willa Cather had been drawn to the composure of Puvis de Chavannes, so Sherwood had been drawn to Van Gogh at the Armory Show. Van Gogh's chairs, towels and pictures on the walls brought back the Mid-Western household scenes and led him to realize these in his short stories, and Van Gogh corroborated the love of vivid colours that one saw in Sherwood's dress and appearance. Sherwood was often in Westport, visiting his brother Karl, the painter who awoke one day feeling that his painting was good for nothing and who then set to work writing a novel. He asked me to revise this novel and I spent a month doing so, rewriting almost every sentence; for Karl, in his effort to avoid the obvious, had used Roget's *Thesaurus*, assuming that synonyms were identical with the words he should have used. As a result the style was blurred, as in a defective colour-print in which the colours do not coincide with the lines; and when I put it in plain English I was astonished to find that Karl had written a Sherwood Anderson story. One afternoon Sherwood himself brought Anita Loos to see us with her husband John Emerson, his old friend. The sprightly author of *Gentlemen Prefer Blondes* seemed very light-hearted that day, little and busy, with her red cap, as a ruby-crowned kinglet.

On another day Robert Frost came to spend the night with us, talking from the moment I met him at two in the afternoon until three o'clock in the morning and then again until five in the afternoon. We had two long walks together and he spoke of his life and adventures, especially his early life in San Francisco. There he had known Henry George, a friend of his father's, and his mother had given him Bellamy's *Looking Backward*, which as a boy he had learned by heart. He had thought of New England then as clam-like and occluded while California was generous and big-hearted. Nobody out there had regarded pennies, and he remembered holding up a nickel and a penny to point out the difference between the regions; the nickel in his mind stood for California and the mean little copper for New England. When he began to write, he felt it was quite noble of him to have discovered that New England was interesting too. But his best time of life was the six years or more when he and his wife had farmed at Derry in New Hampshire, and he had bought another farm near the top of Vermont where he could go for the hay-fever season. He said he had always been too poor to have pictures in the house and he regretted that he had learned little about art now that his daughter had become a sculptor. But he had gone to Ireland to spend a week with AE, who had given him one of his large paintings, a picture that now hung in his house at Amherst. Frost had won the Pulitzer Prize three times; he had a "season ticket," said Hendrik van Loon.

I had first met Robert Frost far up-town in New York and had walked with him six miles down to my hotel. We had then talked until five in the morning, and this was Robert's regular way of making friends, one meeting that lasted all night. His feeling about New England had changed altogether, and when I wrote *The Flowering of New England* he said it was an "emotional experience for me of the highest,—there's a poem out of it, which you must read one day." He had been tempted lately to leave all, he said, and "constitute myself defender of Puritan New England . . . What do you assume it is that makes people like George Santayana, James Truslow Adams and Henry Wallace hate New England,—her having given herself so generously away to the whole country?" But he said he would consign New England to me "while I turn to fight the battles of the Supreme Court of the United States." He had by that time become a reactionary who had no use for Henry George or Bellamy and who was attacking Franklin Roosevelt and his New Deal by way of making amends to his wife. "I dragged her over the stones," he said to me again and again after the death of his wife; she had hated Roosevelt, taking their hard-earned pennies and throwing them away on the riff-raff of the cities; and to turn against Roosevelt was his only way of atoning for the hardships he had caused her. But in that earlier time this companionable man had talked mainly about the country people, the mail-clerk he had known in Vermont and the real-estate man at Amherst; and, with his endless zest for the play of personality, he recalled Sherwood Anderson talking about his neighbours in the South. He said he wished he could have three lives, one to be a failure and see how he behaved through this, one to be an early success and see how he behaved as a later failure, one to be an early failure and see how he behaved as a later success. He had a good-natured scorn for the New York critics and laughed at them for wishing to be "first among the seconds, as we say about the apple barrels"; and he laughed at a certain novelist who was always accusing him of not being on the firing-line. "I fight with a spear," he said. "They fight with dirks. The dirk is the city weapon. I fight from a long way back."

It seemed to me that Frost's strength was that he shared the popular feelings while he made no concessions to the popular mind; and he gave one the fixed impression that America was sound in essence. He was, like Carl Sandburg, a public poet, and again, like Sandburg, Frost wandered all over the country, familiar with Key West and San Antonio, Colorado and Santa Fe, Montana, where one of his daughters lived, Kansas and Texas. Later, when I lunched with him before he set out for Oxford and Dublin, he said the attacks on materialism were all nonsense. Was it not supposed that God materialized himself in Christ? He was all for the material guided by the spiritual, and he said the Oriental mind had withered away because it considered the spiritual alone. Then he laughed at a writer who said that the important thing was, quite simply, to represent the age. In a dull age the greatest man would therefore be the dullest man and in a confused age the greatest mind was the most confused. Frost might have agreed with Pablo Casals who spoke, in his *Conversations,* of atonal music. This music was supposed to be a reflection of the uncertainty of our chaotic period, and Casals said, "Why should an artist be obsessed with the uncertainties of our time instead of reacting against them by showing his faith in those human values which have survived so many collective catastrophes? However dark our times may seem, art should bring a message of hope."

"What an aura that man has about him!" one of my Westport neighbours said about Robert Frost. As a boy in Indiana he had heard Frost, Masters, Sandburg and Lindsay give public readings, and these poets had started him off on his own literary life. Edgar Lee Masters also came out to see us on a mellow October day when we sat under our apple tree and discussed the state of man and his chance of reaching paradise one way or another. Like most of my Mid-Western friends, he thought of me as a New Englander, not troubling to differentiate between the various species of men who had grown up on the Eastern seaboard. This square-faced bespectacled lawyer-poet had a great interest in his forbears in Vermont, and, as for Emerson, his poems and essays delighted Masters. There was scarcely a word of Emerson's with which he did not agree, and he said that an essay could be written on Emerson's saving wisdom to the youth of America for fifty years past. He defended his erratic book on Abraham Lincoln, though he said he could not guess how it would affect his best friends. It had practically alienated Vachel Lindsay.

Robert Frost had known Gamaliel Bradford whose diary and letters I edited in 1932. At the Bradford house in Wellesley Hills, I had met Merrill Moore, the poet who had once been one of the "Fugitives" of Tennessee and who was now a psychiatrist practising in Boston. Merrill Moore asked Mrs. Bradford for the programme of a symphony concert because he saw a sonnet in it, and he wrote another sonnet on a little bronze statue of Shakespeare in the drawing-room where the Wellesley girls had once teased Vachel Lindsay. On his way home Merrill Moore dictated the sonnets to his wife and she wrote them down while he was driving. There was a kind of waffle-iron in Merrill Moore's brain that turned into the shape of a sonnet every thought that entered it, and he was supposed to have written twenty thousand sonnets. Meanwhile, to the neighbourhood of Boston soon came Rudolph Ruzicka whom I had first known during a summer he had spent at Fairfield, near Westport. After this town he had named the lovely Fairfield type that I have since used in all my books, a type that virtually reproduced Rudolph's own handwriting and that he used himself in his little book on Bewick. He greatly admired this old wood-engraver whom Audubon had known and visited in England. Rudolph was cut off from the country of his birth, Bohemia, and he told me that the translation of *Walden,* printed in Prague with his illustrations, had been withheld from distribution pending an investigation of the "ideological merit" of the book. Rudolph liked to quote the Italian proverb, "In conversation it is easy to draw a cheque of erudition on insufficient funds," but there was never a more erudite man than this book-designer who was almost universally cultivated. Living in Dobbs Ferry and then in New York, he felt the lack of a traditional attachment to some place where he could finally belong, and, settling first in Concord, he went to live in Boston.

Of the Westport painters, I knew best Charles Prendergast, a true primitive old master to whom only Vasari could have done justice. He was a reincarnation of the down-east Yankees who carved figureheads for ships, Hawthorne's Drowne, for instance, of the "wooden image"; and his art of gilded figures grew out of his craft as a carver of picture-frames. His mind was like a brook flowing in the woods with leaves floating on it and flowers on the bank. He always reminded me of the Chinese painter Kakki who said that an artist must nourish in his bosom mildness and magnanimity and that only dwelling in a quiet house, in a retired room with the windows open, could he have good feeling for painting and create the Yu. One met at Prendergast's house some of the older painters. Alfred Maurer came there and W. J. Glackens died there, one morning after breakfast while he was smoking a cigar, but one never saw Everett Shinn there, another of the "Eight" who lived in the village behind a high brick wall. Shinn had lost much of his impulse as a painter, though he made occasional illustrations and worked off his energy writing plays. Then, leaving his wife, he lived for a while in a cottage near the cemetery where his telephone, light and water were soon cut off. Shinn, who had made and lost fortunes decorating theatres, would lie on the beach all day in summer, and he read me letters from Poultney Bigelow sent in envelopes franked by the Kaiser, Bigelow's old school-friend in Germany, turned inside out.

Meanwhile, a legacy that came to my wife and me removed one of the causes of my breakdown and enabled me, in this time of depression, to do the work I chose and that alone. For me there was to be no more writing *invita Minerva*. I was able to refuse the positions that were offered me, the literary editorship of *The Sun* and the managing editorship of *The Saturday Review* and *The New Masses*. I was asked to be managing editor of *The Dial*, which had given me its award, and one day, when William Allen White died, I was asked to be one of the judges of the Book-of-the-Month Club. It seemed to me that, in this position, I would be urged to make the most popular book of the month appear to be the best one. Time, not money, Schopenhauer said, is the true treasure of life, and because money bought them time he argued that thinking people should have means ample enough to allow them leisure. How I agreed with Agassiz's saying, "I have no time to waste in making money!" When I thought what financial security was to mean to me,—and this was confirmed after my mother's death, —I could understand how many talents were destroyed without it and how many lives were marred or seriously injured. Paul Rosenfeld's life was crippled by the comparative poverty to which he was reduced during the depression, the generous Paul who was no longer able to help other people as he had once offered to help me. What became of so many of the hopeful and promising young writers whom I had known in the last twenty years? They were frustrated, bitter, forgotten, disappointed, often enough for lack of money, and only occasionally reconciled to an average existence.

I remember a dinner at Paul's later at which E. E. Cummings went off like a geyser of Yankee humour. He told us about the American soldiers in Africa forcing the Africans to be "free," compelling them to be free against their will. Years after this I saw Cummings in Rome and in New York, but I never forgot how that evening he piled one absurdity on another until they reached a towering comic height. Then, in 1936, Dhan Ghopal Mukurji came to spend in Westport a week with me. He wished me to collaborate with him in a book on Yoga, for he felt that he was unequal to presenting the subject in such a way that Americans could understand it. He said that I should relax and permit literature to flow out of my life "like a milk-coloured stream from a rock," and when he gave me lessons in Yoga I sat cross-legged on the floor, trying to evoke the lotus-blossom at the lower end of my spinal column. But one day he said he had been told by his guru that one should not attempt to combine these efforts with intellectual labour. A few weeks after he had stayed with me, Mukurji took his own life, lost as he was between the East and the West.

There was a little indifferent house of which I saw much in the thirties, a house in New Haven, inconspicuous in the street, where lived George Dudley Seymour, an old lawyer. Nothing marked this house but the polished brass knocker and railings by the door; it extended actually, however, a long way at the rear and within were many treasures. There were a dozen portraits of eighteenth-century Connecticut worthies with certain splendid pictures and other works of art, and George Dudley Seymour, whom Sargent had painted, was a Connecticut worthy himself, a genial benefactor of artists and art. He was the chairman of the art commission of the state, and I had first gone to see him about a historical fresco that one of my Westport friends wished to paint. After that he wrote to me, "I am always at home to you at any hour, day or night," and, quoting Governor Winthrop, he called himself "an obscure person content to lie hid among the retired philosophers." Then, "fabulously" old, but "permanently" mine, he was paralysed so that he could not speak, yet, smiling as ever, he promoted the fame of Nathan Hale whose birthplace he bought and put in order.

How many houses I had seen elsewhere, unimportant outside, but full of wonders within, the house of Denman Ross, for instance, the Harvard worthy whom Berenson called "far more subtle, penetrating and serious" than Roger Fry. This little dwelling on a Cambridge "delta" was, as I remember it, one of the finest museums of Oriental art, surprising to me as a certain small house in Westport where an old magazine editor asked me to call upon him. How did they ever get there, the Bronzino portrait and the Tintoretto that covered, with other treasures, the walls of this cottage? I only know that they were acquired, a year or two later, by the Metropolitan Museum in New York. But what struck me in all these houses was something I took for a symbol of an America that travellers seldom see, something remaining amid the "strangeness," the "queerness" of the time, that seemed to me singularly reassuring. They were as private as the lives of Emily Dickinson and Albert Ryder whose motto might have been "Hide thy life," and I could not forget, in an age of space-ships, world wars and publicity, that the real things of the country were hidden and inward.

CHAPTER II

TRAVELS NORTH AND SOUTH

IN THE migrating season of early summer, all the world visited Westport. The intelligentsia fled in a body from New York, and one of our friends said that living in the village then was rather like living in a revolving door. One had to go away to escape from cocktail parties with "sounds that are not voices," as Ellen Glasgow wrote to me from her summer house on the coast of Maine where she looked down on blue water and across blue water to still bluer hills. The country was so fresh there, she said, that it might have been created at dawn and she felt a closer kinship with its clear outlines and green ponds than she felt with her tropical Virginian splendour of bloom. We often drove at that time to Maine where there were no insects to mar the perfect foliage of the oaks and the maples, where there was scarcely a murmur even from the hemlocks and where the ticking of the old wooden clock in the farmhouse that we rented brought back the odours and the flavours of a hundred years ago. It gave one the feeling of space and time, of clarity, simplicity and amplitude that vanished in the feverish summer time at home.

No one conveyed this feeling of an immemorial American scene as well as Henry Beston at Nobleboro on the northern farm he described in a beautiful book that rebuked the impoverished language of everyday writers. A prose Robert Frost, an artist in words, Henry Beston continued to live in a world of country handicrafts and bright colours, plaid shirts and heavy caps of red, green and blue, where the people caned chairs, hooked rugs and whittled playthings as in the time of Thoreau or of Currier and Ives. He had a great herb garden; he even had a mandrake that had been brought from the Valley of Armageddon; and he read agricultural magazines in which he said sound English continues in our abstract civilization. I could understand, reading him, the vogue of Gertrude Stein, in a world of journalistic clichés and academic jargon, for she seemed to make words new by destroying their context. Henry Beston, with his country lore, rehumanized the American scene in which human beings had become vagrants in space. Moreover, his book seemed to be alive with the creatures of the forest and the sea, gulls, curlews, hawks, deer, the wildcat and the moose. In *The Outermost House,* about Cape Cod, he evoked the great elemental sounds, the sound of rain, the sound of wind in a primeval wood and the sound of the outer ocean on a beach; and, half French himself, in his book on the Saint Lawrence, he recalled the habitants whom he had known upon this river. They did not merely use but cherished the land. Remembering the virtues of the native roots and leaves, Henry Beston loved the old wisdom of the American forest.

Henry Beston fully expressed the savour that Maine had for me, just as he expressed Quebec where a professor whom we knew collected the folk stories of the habitants and their songs. This man, the son of a country doctor who had driven all over the province, played for us on his gramophone some of the ancient ballads and tales that had survived on the

Gaspé from the Middle Ages, tales that were often grim and ballads, once gay in France, that had become sinister and heavy in these far-away forests. But Henry Beston, above all, suggested the feeling of Cape Cod, where I lived for many weeks at one time or another, and Martha's Vineyard especially, that wilder Isle of Wight where I had spent a summer once in England. Martha's Vineyard had the same shape and the same dimensions as the Isle of Wight, with little towns set about in corresponding corners, and with moors, cliffs and a "gay head" at the end. It was a world of beaches, wild roses and bay, where at the opening of our sandy road Thomas Hart Benton lived and Francis Hackett came for frequent visits. There also came a friend of my Tahitian brother-in-law, Vilhjalmur Stefansson, who had found the Arctic friendly and who told me that Ole Rölvaag was all wrong in his account of the monotony of the prairie country. It was supposed that the asylums there were full of people who had lost their minds because of the monotony of the prairie landscape, but Stefansson said this was not true at all. He had grown up on the prairie and loved it, though he said it was easier to love mountains and forests because novels and poems had been mostly written in rolling or rugged country and people had been conditioned to prefer it. But the great man of Martha's Vineyard, for me, was Roger Baldwin, an American of the pre-war type who had a special connection with New England, a defender of the under-dog who had thriven before fatalism and cynicism destroyed the general interest in human causes. Along with the Civil Liberties Union, which he had fathered and led, he shared the old rural concern with plants and birds, and every year, in the loft of his barn, he banded the newly-hatched offspring of a great owl that spent the summer there. I know that there still exists a great army of "bird lovers," as numerous as the Mormons or any other sect, and I remember one occasion on Martha's Vineyard when a pair of purple gallinules suddenly appeared there. The telephone wires burned with the news, just as they burned when the word went about that a Carolina warbler had been seen in the woods. Later, in a Connecticut village where an English robin appeared one day, a delegation went out from Hartford to report it.

I have long believed that the best writers are now the writers of natural history who are ignored commonly in critical circles because they are concerned with permanent things outside the changing human world that interests the novelists and most of the poets. From the point of view of the critics they are off-centre, as they were not in the rural past when farmers, ministers and statesmen knew their forest world and wrote about it. Jonathan Edwards at twelve years old produced a long description of the "wondrous way of the working of the forest spider." But intellectual city-dwellers determine the climate of literature now, and beautiful writing scarcely counts in critical circles any longer when it deals with the facts and shows of nature. Otherwise there would be no writers more critically esteemed than Henry Beston or Rachel Carson or Loren Eisley, who has related, in *The Immense Journey*, the ascent of man from his dark stairwell. Why are these writers of natural history now called popularizers of science as if all their style went for nothing, as if theirs were the bottom rung of the ladder of science instead of an upper rung of the ladder of art? Wondering about this, I remembered a remark that Matisse made to Walter Pach, "There are times when even very great artists are unacceptable to us because we are pursuing some line of development in which they have no place." How much truer this is of not-so-great artists and writers who deal, in an urban world, with immutable themes.

In the winter we sometimes went south, and one seemed to enter history the moment one crossed the Potomac; for there were old ladies in Alexandria or in Charleston or St. Augustine who opened abysses in the dark backward of time. They told stories about the Civil War that never appeared in the history books, and one old lady at Warrenton remembered the battle of Bull Run and how Generals Pope and McClellan had advanced on the town. Pope had sent word that he would make his headquarters in her family's house, but, knowing his ferocious reputation, they had sent word to General McClellan, asking him to stay with them. When he came,—they had known him in Washington,—he treated them with great consideration, and General Pope was obliged to take a house down the hill. On the battlefield itself, eighty years after the battle, a ragged old man hurried out to guide us. He had been a boy of nine, he had watched the fighting from the Henry house, and "My goodness," he exclaimed, "I wish I could remember things that happened yesterday as well as I remember that day." He had been a helper in the little stone hospital, and he saw the surgeons cutting off hundreds of arms and legs and piling them under a big tree he pointed out.

In these old Southern towns life seemed to have stood still, and I could understand the Southern renaissance of the moment when so many folk legends and myths were still alive there. In the South much of the past survived in the present. I shaved in the morning in Alexandria in the same small mirror that George Washington was supposed to have used for shaving, bought, with the dinner-plates we also used, at the auction in Mount Vernon where the last Washington had lived, a bankrupt. Then, on a rainy night in Kentucky, I watched an old blind ballad-singer, a humble reincarnation of Beowulf and Homer, sitting on a bench with his guitar waiting for a bus while he improvised a ballad on a recent murder.

I remember a lady in Charleston saying, "Lafayette sat *right here*," as she pointed to the left-hand corner of a sofa; and I remember two old ladies who lived in a large house with a sign "Rooms to Let" affixed to the wall. Over the entrance was a massive wrought-iron grille,—a battered marble capital surmounted each of the lofty gate-posts,—and when I rang the bell at the gate an old Negro appeared in a white coat and held out a Sheffield card-tray as he opened the gate. Then over the long flagstones of the garden he bowed us to the front door where two old sisters stood, desperately eager, obviously, to rent their bedrooms. One of them had learned the correct sales-patter, which she delivered in a halting voice, while the other stood by, with Medusa-like hair, silently consumed with shame and rage, having to open their door to these vandals from the North. We were obliged to enter the dilapidated mansion with Chippendale chairs covered with dust, portraits black with dirt, great pieces of silver dim with mould and fine old rugs stained and tattered; but I had a feeling that there was murder in this house and that we might not have survived a night upstairs.

One of my mother's cousins had married the minister of the Huguenot church, a French Episcopalian clergyman, and he had given us letters to one or two old families, with whom the word "cousin" had a magical effect. You had only to remark in a drawing-room that you were somebody's cousin for a pleasant murmur to go round the room, as if to say, How nice! "Will you have a little Gentleman's Relish?" one of these ladies asked, as she poured a cup of tea for me. Another lady showed us, among the early tombstones, where an angel or a death's-head would commonly be, a medallion of an eighteenth-century belle, carved in the stone in her evening gown, as if she were going out to dinner. "Of course," this lady said to me, "We do feel we're a little different." They had had, for a few years, in South Carolina, a provincial house of peers, with four orders of nobility, landgraves, margraves, barons and one other, which had been recognized by the British House of Lords. Eighteenth-century Charleston was a far-away outpost of London, and I saw, in the Goose Creek church-yard, the tombstone of a lawyer who had "set the table on a roar." One could see, in DuBose Hayward's *Mamba's Daughters,* the efforts the Charlestonians made to maintain, in a fluid world, their position in society, as if, like King Canute holding back the ocean, to stop the fluidity that was washing them out.

Charleston struck me as a school of manners, not least among the Negroes, the "quality coloured folks" who were "raised with *ways";* and they told me on Folly Island about George Gershwin's cousin, the painter, who had written home that he could hardly work there. He was too disturbed by the "bellowing of the alligators and the shouts and cries of the wild blacks," the Uncle Toms and Dinahs who inhabited the island. I remember an old postman with a goatee and an air of General Beauregard who took off his hat to me with a ceremonious bow, and a policeman who was so polite when I parked my car in the wrong place and who quietly hastened after me. He refrained from saying, "Hey, Jack, what's the idea?" Instead of this greeting of the North, he remarked to me in a gentle voice, "Excuse me, sir, I think," etc., etc. But some of the Negroes had to choose between light and heat in their cabins. They had no glass windows but only wooden shutters, and so when they started a fire for cooking they had to close the shutters and live and cook in the dark to keep the heat in. When they opened the shutters to get light, they were obliged to let the fire go out.

In Richmond, coming or going, we saw Ellen Glasgow now and then in the big square grey brick house, with magnolia and holly around it, where she had written all her novels. I had wondered at Sinclair Lewis's remark one day to me, "Can you read Ellen Glasgow? I can't and Willa Cather says she can't either." At that time Sinclair Lewis was living on Central Park West. He saw much of Willa Cather who lived across the park and, as I gathered, saw almost no one else. Was Ellen Glasgow possibly too tame for Sinclair Lewis and too domesticated for Willa Cather, in whom might well have lingered unhappy associations with the Virginia of Ellen Glasgow's novels? I could not understand their distaste for this fine work any more than the statement of a "formalist" critic, who was himself a Southerner, that Ellen Glasgow's novels were "journalistic." She had "style" but no "form," this writer contended, and she could no longer be read when critics "had come to expect a novel to be what good novels had always been, as formally perfect as a poem." *What* novels? I said to myself. Was *Wuthering Heights* formally perfect, or anything of Dickens, Balzac or Dostoievsky? In any case, was it not more important that the author of *The Sheltered Life* was the turning-point in the literary history of the South? She told me in Richmond about a picnic when she was six or seven at which she had eaten a ham sandwich; picking out the fat, she had thrown it away, saying "I never could abide fat!" She had always felt that way, as any reader of her novels could see, and it was Ellen Glasgow who had destroyed the taste for fat in the Southern literary mind.

But no doubt the distaste for Ellen Glasgow of the later Southern writers, or at least of the formalist critics who were mostly Southern, was that she had seen the old South as it really was instead of the idealized South of *I'll Take My Stand*. The Southern revival had begun with minds like hers or like the mind of the philosopher of North Carolina, Thomas Wolfe's "last of the heroes," Horace Williams, who had said, "The Saviour was not a Methodist." Horace Williams had broken the grip of the Southern fundamentalists, just as Ellen Glasgow hated and exposed the "inherent falseness" in much of the Southern tradition; and the agrarians had revived the old fundamentalist orthodoxy along with a romantic view of the antebellum South. No wonder the "new" critics ignored or patronized her, and all the more because she was interested in the creation of character and because she wrote social history or the history of manners, irrelevant interests from their point of view. Ellen Glasgow called herself "a Southerner, though a recalcitrant one," but there was no doubt that she loved Virginia, as we could see when she drove us all over the country of *Barren Ground*. She took us to lunch at the president's house in Williamsburg and to Westover, Claremont Manor and Upper Brandon.

"Oh, Ellen's too full of herself!" Mrs. Charles Dana Gibson said to me when I first met this typical Southern belle, one of the belles and beauties whom Ellen Glasgow knew so well and whom in one book or another she so admirably pictured. Mrs. Gibson had given me one side of her cocktail glass, by way of a loving-cup, in the fashion of a belle. Ellen Glasgow *was* too full of herself, but in that bland Richmond world how could she have carried on if she had *not* been, if she had not barricaded herself and defended her great interest by nursing an anti-social rebellious ego? She once spoke of James Branch

Cabell as having survived "the blighting frustration of every artist in the South," in Richmond where everyone looked with suspicion on what they called "people who write" and no one had any sympathy with her inclinations. She told me that when she was young she had filled an Indian basket with the letters of her first publisher, Walter H. Page,—my own first chief in a far-off day in New York,—and that when she was away from home her sister had burned these cherished letters and used the basket for her own Red Cross knitting. I remembered the complaint of Thomas Nelson Page about the destruction of old family papers that made it so difficult to write the history of the South. He said in one of his essays, "The very proofs of our identity and position have been disregarded and destroyed"; and Ellen told me that as a child, on rainy days at Reveille, she and her friends had burned the old papers in the attic. They had carried down armfuls of her family's love-letters of the eighteenth and even the seventeenth century and laughed over them before they put them in the grate, a way people had, she said, in old Southern houses. The interest of history and literature was the last thing to be thought of in a world that knew only gossip and oratory, and no one saw in it the touch of Greek tragedy, Ellen Glasgow said, when the story of the incest of the Randolphs came to light. The only comment of the Richmond people was, "Why rake up that old scandal?"

When later I told Stark Young that I hoped to write about the South, he replied that "Southern history and the general Southern quality have a curiously illusive essence, almost impossible to define . . . Some critics in New York took *So Red the Rose* as a romance, when it laboriously expresses,— in terms of images and creation, I hope,—a great many Southern traits." I had no doubt that Stark Young was right and that the "illusive essence" was partly a result of the absence of documents and facts, while it was related to the kind of poetry one found in Savannah, for instance, in the Bonaventure cemetery and its overgrown tombs. The long cypress alleys and the camellias blossoming under the Spanish moss, so redolent of *Ulalume* and *Annabel Lee*, brought back an old South that was more poetic than anything else in America, even than Gothic Salem or the Hudson river. I could understand Henry Miller's rhapsody over Louisiana and the colour and warmth bequeathed by the great old plantations to the brief and bleak pattern of our historical life, and I could see why New Orleans had supplanted Boston as a focus of literary interest. Especially when the "bad girl," who was supposed to have abounded there, became a favourite theme of American fiction, but more when the genius of Faulkner evoked a school of followers all over that region of the South.

CHAPTER III

IN THE WEST

Y EARS LATER, at Big Sur, I fell in with Henry Miller in his camp-life nest on a ridge overlooking the Pacific. Deep at that time in my literary history, I was eager to see the country, and I had returned for two or three winters to Carmel where I had been married in 1911. Thirty miles south of the village, one could almost have tossed a stone from Henry Miller's cabin into the ocean. There was a glass door at the rear that Miller had painted with symbolic designs expressing his great care for the esoteric, and on a rock outside stood a porcelain bathtub equipped for ablutions in the wind and sun. An anarchist still, he seemed to have outlived the mood of *The Tropic of Cancer,* that "kick in the pants to God, man, destiny, time, love, beauty"; and he wore about his neck a Yemenite amulet, a small silver disk, that his Jewish brother-in-law had given him. He had the air of an aging Buddhist monk, and this lover of romantic mystery and all things arcane to whom America *in toto* was an air-conditioned nightmare had found on the California coast some of the feeling that in Greece had made *The Colossus of Maroussi* the best of his books. He had become a Zen Buddhist, like some of the Beatniks who had found their way already to his high ridge.

I had driven out through the Middle West, and through the Southwest, where there were still people who spoke the old Spanish of Cervantes. I had seen a village of the Stone Age across the Rio Grande, from a twentieth century highway in El Paso, and then one came to the Casa Grande, a huge ceremonial building erected at the same time as the cathedral of Chartres. There were the living pueblos, Acoma and Taos, and there was the tomb of Percival Lowell with its visible sarcophagus under the great dome of bluish glass. I had seen nothing so romantic and dramatic since I had spent a week near the lonely tomb of Chateaubriand on the coast of Brittany. There had been, a few years before, a literary movement at Santa Fe, and there was much weaving at handlooms now while adobe houses were still going up and local poets went in for Indian song-poems. The Southwest and California might have been another country; they were like a northern Chile or Peru; but, as a part of the United States, they extended almost indefinitely its memory and tradition of literature and art. The first wagon had entered this territory in the very year in which Shakespeare wrote *The Merchant of Venice,* and I was shown a madonna that was painted near Los Angeles when Leonardo da Vinci was still living. All the European epochs were jostled together in the United States, the Middle Ages in the Kentucky blood-feuds, the eighteenth century in Charleston and in Taos prehistoric time.

It struck me on the road that my fellow-countrymen were perhaps the strangest people in the world. I mean the common run who think they are the only normal folk and that all the rest are wops or chinks or dagoes. I watched them in their cars from New Jersey to Missouri, and they seemed to be unable to eat except to the accompaniment of the raucous strains of a radio singing about LUV. They ate at any hour that appealed

to their fancy, with the odour of cheap fried fat heavy on the
air, shakes and burgers, French fries, hot dogs and Seven-Up
mixed, in any sequence, all together. They grabbed their grub
and took it out to devour in their mobile caves to the sound
of "Busy Body Boogie," "That Crazy Mambo Thing" and
"Teach Me Tonight," and it seemed to me that we were the
most uncivilized people on earth, though no doubt also the most
solicitous and kind; for when, at a roadside café, they said,
"How are you this evening, folks?" one sometimes felt that this
greeting came from the heart. The phrase "a real American"
meant, in the West, as I found, simply a liberal, honest and
unprejudiced man: it had none of the sinister overtones with
which the intellectuals whom I had known at home invested it.
But was the word "Easterner" still a magic word there? A friend
in Chicago had written to me, an Easterner himself, "I assure
you that an Easterner is always suspect here. They think that
we think we are superior and dare us to patronize them." He
said the Middle West still seemed unsure of itself and always
"feared its slip might be showing," unlike the self-confident
Far West where I remembered, nevertheless, the prestige the
word "Easterner" had when I had first gone there. The mere
fact that I was a Harvard man, although I had no advanced
degree, procured for me at once a post in one of the universities.
But that day had long passed in Los Angeles, at Stanford and
in Berkeley.

Now, twenty or thirty years later, I saw, in Los Angeles,
streets named after men I had known in that earlier time,
Gayley Avenue, Hilgard Street and especially Wilshire Boulevard named after Gaylord Wilshire, who had lived in London.
Professor Gayley, the charming Irishman who kept open house
in Berkeley and whom I had seen so often in 1911, had introduced me one afternoon to the great Professor Hilgard, who

stopped for a moment to speak on Channing Way. Remembering, along with the author of Gayley's *Classic Myths,* this fine
old man's face and bearing, I realized, seeing these two names
on street signs in Los Angeles, what a long generation had gone
by. When I went to England to teach in 1913, I had seen a good
deal of Gaylord Wilshire in his old house on Hampstead Heath
where, on Sunday afternoons, lions, lionesses and cubs of all
degrees assembled. One day Mrs. Wilshire said to me, "Our
afternoons are always distinctive. We never know what the
symposium will be. Today, you see, it is spooks." One man
there had written a story about a woman who was pestered by
Frank R. Stockton's ghost, and one of the spooks was a "miracle
girl" supposed to have been dying of three diseases when an
angel appeared and told her to arise and walk. This young lady
rebuked me for killing a spider on the hearthstone.

In Los Angeles I met Lion Feuchtwanger, who had lived for
eleven years in his walled garden, although every day his wife
sent him out for a walk up the steep hill outside. Meeting few
Americans, and having escaped from the Nazis, he was convinced that he was surrounded with wolves, that America was
run by an Ogpu while the Russians were free. In his dream of
the Middle Ages, about which he was writing historical novels,
he had scarcely caught a whiff of the real air about him; and he
was so used to being a best-seller that not to be taken by the
Book-of-the-Month Club was, he felt, not to be published at
all. Besides history, his reading consisted mainly of bookseller's
catalogues from all quarters of the world; he put his money
into first editions, and there were in his house hundreds of
shelves with complete original sets of Goethe, Rousseau, Field-
ing, Milton and others. He had a Shakespeare folio and an
edition of Spinoza with the philosopher's own annotations. The
garden from which had been gathered that year eleven thousand

bananas, he said, overlooked a Hindu shrine, a few hundred yards below, in which were buried some of Gandhi's ashes.

I spent an afternoon near Los Angeles, where he lived, with that good and most lovable man, Upton Sinclair, who, in a time of great talents with small hearts, had, it seemed to me, a particularly large one. He stood at the gate of his big Spanish house with the sun beating down,—there were no trees, there was nothing to shade it,—and, on this bright spring day, he received me in a darkened room with all the window-shades closely drawn. Deeply shrouded electric lamps, with bowls of pink camellias, stood in every corner of the room, while his wife, who was scarcely able to move, so frail her heart was, sat in the semi-darkness like a heroine of Poe. He told me that he had prepared for her six hundred pots of rice that year, no new thing for this old believer in experimental diets. At the rear, out in the sun, he showed me two storehouses of corrugated iron, filled with translations of his books in forty-seven languages. Years before, I had written an article saying that I did not like these books and could not believe in them from any point of view, but this statement never satisfied me, especially in recent years when I had a deep feeling of kinship with Sinclair. I was drawn to him all the more when the literary tide turned away from everything we had in common.

I had been judging him by the ordinary scale of novelists, whose material, he said, they collected with a microscope whereas he collected his with a telescope. There was no use in observing that novels are about individuals when he said that institutions were "higher products of evolution," and, when he wrote that he was "impatient of every form of stupidity," why reply that this was not the attitude of a novelist? Upton Sinclair's characters lived only as political minds, they existed only in political views and relations, in what they thought and said, not in what they were. Sinclair had always used fiction for ulterior purposes, and this was the cause of the quarrel between him and the critics. But, although he did not fit into any of the usual categories, he was obviously something on a large scale; and this explained why, in spite of the critics, he interested Einstein and Bernard Shaw, Gandhi, Georg Brandes and Bertrand Russell. He had a passion for improving life and the world.

With Will Durant I also spent an afternoon, the gentle philosopher-scholar in whose study I saw the account-books that contained the two draughts he had written of all his historical volumes. Like Sinclair, he was a lovable man, with his quiet wisdom, and I reflected on comments I had heard that this rare student was a popularizer of other men's discoveries and thoughts. What's in a name? I asked myself. In our servile world of scholarship, a man who is called "Will" instead of "William" cannot get the respect he surely deserves; for this writer was a formidable savant without any question. I was struck by his explanation of the idea of original sin, and the firm grip it had acquired over the human intellect. He thought it was a survival of the prehistoric day when men killed one another in order to survive, an act that became murder in a changed civilization when men had become aware of good and evil. An aberration of the days of innocence, before men had achieved the moral sense, it had suffused with a permanent sense of guilt the collective unconscious.

In old times, at Carmel, where she was already legendary, I had seen much of Mary Austin, who had written *The Flock, Lost Borders* and *The Land of Little Rain*, beautiful evocations of the life of the desert. Having lived among the Indians in the Southwest, she thought of herself as a medicine-woman, a priestess, an inspired leader of the tribe, and she felt the fury of the woman scorned because she was not recognized by the

Americans who were her own tribe. Among these were the
"New York critics," as she called them, who could not accept
her theories of the American rhythm, the American experience,
the American literary form, derived, as she supposed, from the
"first Americans, the Indians," with whom she felt our culture
was organically connected. In New York, she was always looking for slights, always on the defensive, she became a *femme
incomprise*, the "lonely disappointed woman with an empress
complex"; for, after writing these fine books, she never found a
subject she was at home with. But at Carmel, among her old
friends, the chip disappeared from her shoulder, and she was
sometimes like an old gypsy fortune-teller, reading the cards
and distributing good-luck emblems. She gave me a talisman,
covered with Indian signs, a pair of horns and a pine-tree in
water-colour, and she sent me some "glyphs," or Amerind poems,
in which an object, suddenly seen, fires a train of associations.
But she had as many delusions as her people in *Lost Borders*
whose minds melted away in the mirages of the desert. She had
gone to Rome in 1907 to study Catholic mysticism, in preparation for her book *The Man Jesus*, and she had applied at
the Vatican for someone to give her instruction in Catholic
doctrine. Cardinal Merry del Val himself had volunteered, she
told me, to give her his personal instruction, and she was convinced that, after four or five hours they had spent together,
he had fallen in love with her. At that point she had hurried
away from Rome.

One evening on the beach, we had a picnic party for Mary
Austin. We knew nothing of the Carmel feuds, the quarrels
that divided the artists and writers, numbers of whom for years
had refused to speak to one another. We asked indiscriminately
all whom we knew and wondered at the embarrassments and
hesitations that were evident when the people began to appear.

But many feuds, I think, were composed that night, for Mary Austin brought them all together. She was in her element sitting by a camp-fire, which called out all her gifts of story-telling. She told her story of Vasquez and the white horse, regarding which she had no doubts whatever. Vasquez was a Mexican bandit who had lived at Carmel in a little cabin in the San José canyon. We often walked up the canyon to this ruined cabin, round which wild Easter lilies grew, strays, I suppose, from some old garden. Vasquez had had a white horse, which was famous all over the country, for he used to ride this horse up and down the highway that ran between Los Angeles and San Francisco. His specialty was robbing the mail-coach. Finally Vasquez was captured and hanged and his white horse was shot, but the ghost of the horse still haunted the highway, and it always happened that whenever the horse appeared the driver of the mail-coach was killed shortly afterward. Mary Austin had seen this ghost of the white horse. She was riding all night on the mail-coach, sitting beside the driver, and just before dawn, in the darkness, the white horse suddenly appeared trotting along beside the others. Mary Austin had been collecting peach pits, which were used for making munitions in the war, and she had in her lap a bag of these peach pits, which she threw, one by one, on the back of the horse. As long as she could see them bounce off its back, she knew that the horse was there and not an illusion. Then, suddenly, as day broke, the white horse vanished. There was no bush, wall or tree behind which it could have disappeared, for they were driving across an open plain. The horse simply dissolved in the air. On its return journey northward, the stage met with an accident and the driver was killed.

In Westport, one day in the late thirties, I had heard a knock at the front door, and there, when the door opened, stood a man dressed all in black with a shabby little suitcase on the floor beside him. He said he had walked from California, working in the hay-fields, and he asked me for socks and underclothes and, more than that, he wondered if I would give him a shack on my place to live in. He told me that John Steinbeck had put him up on his Western ranch while he wrote two chapters of a novel he had brought with him. I had no such shack on my village half-acre or anything to be compared with John Steinbeck's supposedly great open spaces, but I gladly gave the wanderer the underclothes and socks and offered to read the two chapters of his novel. They seemed to me extremely good, in the style of Hemingway, and I wrote at once to a friend in New York at one of the publishing houses, asking him to give this blackshirt a weekly allowance. He would probably finish in a few months the novel he called *The Middle Way*. My friend arranged to do so, impressed as much as I was by the literary character of these two chapters; but after about six weeks the wanderer disappeared and nothing more was heard of him in New York or elsewhere. He had not added a line to the two chapters, and I wondered if he had really written them.

In Carmel, or rather in Monterey, Steinbeck said he had known this man, and, having read the two chapters, he agreed that they were as remarkable as I had thought them; but the writer had suddenly vanished, and Steinbeck himself supposed that he had copied them out of some published novel. Steinbeck was living in an old adobe house which he had hoped to own when he was a boy; he had just bought this Casa de Soto and planned to spend all the year there, though he worked in the directors' room at the Monterey bank. There was a large living-room, white, with a stove of coloured tiles made for him by Henry Varnum Poor, a big Mexican painting by Sequiros, a wall of books, a bedroom and a primitive kitchen at the rear.

Behind the house was a small garden with rich black earth where Steinbeck had just planted spinach, onions and carrots. Then there was a huge cactus plant with a four-foot trunk that clambered all over the little enclosure. Steinbeck cut off two cactus pears, one yellow and one red, opened them and gave us the hearts.

Steinbeck struck me as big, lively, genial and shrewd. He had a large red face with an upturned nose, and, somehow, the air of a German longshoreman. He said that Monterey was the only small town that was not like a small town: you could do anything there and nobody cared if you did not interfere with other people. It was, on a tiny scale, a cosmopolitan city, but he had been refused a working room in the so-called Professional Building because he could not convince the manager that he was a serious working-man. It seemed to please him that the manager did not know who he was, there in little Monterey. I thought he was established for life there, but a year later, passing the house, I saw at the door a moving-van, and I knew that Steinbeck was on the wing once more.

Sinclair Lewis asked me once what sort of man Steinbeck was, for Lewis had never seen him and knew little about him, and it struck me then that we had no community of literature, such as we had had in the nineteenth century and even later. The writers at that time had all known one another, but now they were as solitary as the rhinoceros roaming the veldt or as lone wolves drifting about a wilderness, and I remembered Sherwood Anderson's proposal that they should write to one another and form in that way some sort of relation. Steinbeck said that he knew Robinson Jeffers very slightly, although he regarded him as a great writer, and he thought that Jeffers had stopped writing because he had entered the real world for which his mind was unprepared. He had known the region of the Big

Sur even longer than Jeffers, for his mother had once been a school-teacher there; but the two had little in common in their points of view. Una Jeffers, asking me if I had met Steinbeck, said she did not really like his books,—he had written a novel that was full of sympathy for the lettuce-pickers, but with no feeling for the owners, and that was not life as she and her husband knew it. For the rest, she said she loved the fog of the Shetland Islands, which made her feel that she was alive. Both she and Jeffers hated the sunlight they lived in, and Jeffers said it was poisonous for him.

There was a flock of white pigeons perching all over Tor House on the day when I met Frieda Lawrence there. She had brought her well-known lover, Captain Angelo Ravagli, who had once been a bersagliere; and, with her big friendly voice and shapeless cotton dress, she looked like the grandmother of all the valkyries. I could believe what she said to one of my friends, "Where I am, there is life!" She remarked that her Taos neighbour Brett had just gone to England, wearing a sombrero, high boots, corduroy trousers and a long stiletto tucked in her right stocking, and that Brett's brother, Viscount Esher, said, "For my part, whenever I see her coming, I dive into the nearest shop." At the rear of the house, Jeffers had planted a pine and eucalyptus grove, and, when Frieda Lawrence arrived, I saw down the alley the well-known love-dance of the pheasants. A very gorgeous wild cock pheasant was circling round the tree-trunks, with three hens performing in regular rhythm, and another visitor exclaimed, "What a coincidence when Frieda and her lover have just come here!"

CHAPTER IV

THE OLDER GENERATION

THOUGH I never sought out older writers, or introduced my-self to them, I fell in, early or late, with many of them, sometimes at the end of their lives when they had outlived their vogue and were even more or less broken by the pressures of life. Years before, I had interviewed Howells, I had seen Mark Twain lying in state and I had observed Henry James lecturing at Harvard and later listening to Georg Brandes at a lecture in London. Then I had seen Mary E. Wilkins, a with-ered brown little old woman in a garish dress and hat, receiving a medal at the Academy of Arts and Letters, and Edmund Clarence Stedman, the poet, the translator of Theocritus, at a performance of the *Ajax* of Sophocles. With his fan-shaped beard and dapper little figure, he was leaning over the balcony in a hall where some Greeks were acting on the lower East Side. At Sanders Theatre in Cambridge, when Henry James lectured on Balzac, I had seen the old Western poet Joaquin Miller pushing his way into the front row of seats, and one day, at the Academy, Edwin Markham suddenly appeared, sup-posedly out of his mind, in charge of an attendant. Eighty-eight years old, he had a wild look, and, catching sight of Hamlin Garland, he called out over the heads of the crowd, "What are you doing here with all these dressed-up people?"

No doubt many of these older writers, whether great or small, felt like "flattened balloons, once gayly buoyant," as Robert Grant, the Boston novelist, said to me that he felt, adding, "No man can hope to bridge two generations." Alert as he was at eighty-seven,—he took three steps at a time bounding up an old belvedere when I saw him at Nahant,—he was still young in his feelings and tastes and responded very heartily when I sent him *The Enormous Room* of E. E. Cummings. He said the portraits were "hideously graphic" and that in some ways the book had "Dante's Hell beaten by a mile"; but who remembered at that time his own *The Chippendales* and *Unleavened Bread* that were almost equal to Cummings in their power of satire? Howells, who died in 1920, remarked somewhere that "history is an unwilling guest in our unmemoried land." The author of a hundred books who had been writing for fifty years, he had received one day an invitation from a "home correspondence school" to take lessons in story-writing.

I had been obsessed with the chaos of our American world and the stories of remarkable men who had been forgotten, and I was so conscious of our own shortcomings that I did not realize then how often great artists were misprized in other countries. In seventeenth-century Holland, as Hendrik van Loon reminded me, Franz Hals was forced into bankruptcy while Rembrandt was starving; the greatest genius in the language, Vondel, was a broken-down clerk, and the painters Ruysdael and Hobbema were poor and driven. Even in England, important writers were neglected and lost almost as they were in our indifferent country. Who remembered Ralph Hodgson, effaced on a farm in Minerva, Ohio, where he was running a dog-kennel? One day I received a letter from Dame Katherine Furse, who hoped to write something about her father, John Addington Symonds. I had written a juvenile book on Symonds, and Dame Katherine Furse asked me if I knew in America any friends of her father's: could I put her on the track of any material about him? "After he died," she said, "it was as though the sea had closed over him": in all England only Havelock Ellis remembered her father and could tell her anything about him. I was able to give her the names of three American friends of Symonds who had letters of his and memories of him.

One of these friends was Thomas Sergeant Perry,—"the poor dear consistently pessimistic Tom Perry," as Henry James called him in a letter to Howells. A friend of James also from boyhood and the first translator of Turgenev, whom he had introduced to both James and Howells, he had written to me to praise my life of Symonds and continued to write for many years thereafter. "I never have a chance to talk on these subjects with anyone here," for Boston, he said, "is not a literary centre. Until very recently I would pursue Howells with talk, but now I am innocuous for lack of victims"; and he was pessimistic indeed about the state of American letters,—"how scanty and voiceless and self-conscious that literature is," he said, writing at the beginning of the twenties. "In a country not yet formed, only forming itself, there is no soil for literature. No one in this country has any roots anywhere; we don't live in America, we board here, we are like spiders that run over the surface of the water." He enjoyed my old paper *The Freeman*, detesting the political part of it, saying, "Almost all the writers have a revolution in their pockets"; but he remarked, "You have, I think, the best literary journal in the country," if only we would stop chanting about the desirability of an American literature. "I am almost as sick of the two words as I am of 'old glory,' which makes me shudder and feel unclean . . . You can't get a literature by whistling for it any more than you can get a crop of asparagus by laying down the bed six months before the spring when you want it . . . A mould is slowly forming in which time may bring something up, but remember how long it was before Rome got to work and really how small the crop. I think of the long time it took Germany to get to work, and the vastness of Russia and the little produced so far." In a similar vein George Santayana wrote to me about our cultural ferment of the nineteen-twenties, "It is veneer, rouge, aestheticism, art-museums, new theatres, etc., that make America impotent. The good things are football, kindness and jazz bands." Every day Perry went to the Boston Public Library, where later a bronze memorial tablet was erected to his memory; and he wrote that he sat where all the new books were displayed and could see how few of them were worth looking at. He had lived through the dry decades of the post-Civil War time, and perhaps he would not have liked the new books of the twenties when it seemed to the young that everything was beginning again just as it had seemed in the time of Emerson and Hawthorne.

To this grandson of Commodore Perry the world was "going straight to Hell," but he was full of alert curiosity about the Russians and the French and he was a lover especially of Chekhov. He had seen *The Cherry Orchard* in Petrograd in 1908, and as an old translator he was shocked by the version of a Yale instructor "whose English was that of a Chicago street barbarian. . . . If you are in or near New York, sell your last shirt," he wrote to me, "and see the Moscow Art Company in one of Chekhov's plays. . . . Never again will you see such acting, of that you may be certain." (In fact, I never saw an actor to compare with Moskvin, who, sitting before the curtain, acted the part of a switchman on a railroad. Although he spoke in Russian and I did not know a word of Russian, I seemed to understand every word he said.) Perry had turned up some early letters that Henry James had written to him from Bonn and Geneva in 1859 and 1860: they were in a very delicate and fragile state, something like that of the manuscripts at Herculaneum that had been so tenderly uncovered. Perry had been spending the winter on a sugar plantation in Louisiana, but he had known James when they were boys at Newport, and he remembered when *Le Comte Kostia* came out,—"We put the number of the *Revue* into a sailboat and set off on an all-day trip. . . . All of H.J.'s previous life was tinctured with the Gallic juices, Balzac, Georges Sand, Cherbuliez, Musset, they were all at work on the James family." When I was translating Gauguin's hand-written journal, and no doubt complaining about it, he said many painters wrote abominably, but Monet's writing was very clear and Pissarro's was like copperplate,— "his manuscript lay in the middle of a page like one egg in a nest." Perry, who had lived in France, had known both Pissarro and Monet, and he said that Monet and Emerson were the most memorable men he had ever met: they had deeply impressed him with their power. Over the Sage of Concord he had "gently giggled" in 1862 with Henry James and his brother William, but he said that Emerson had "the divine spark and it flashed at times through the scoriae." In France he had met Zola and gone to a Magny dinner with Edmond de Goncourt. "I got the impression of having dined in a pirate's cave," he said, almost in the words of Henry James.

Then, one day, Mrs. Perry wrote to me. Eager to defend old Cambridge and Boston, she wished to explain to me why Henry James had found them "deadly,"—it was not the places themselves "but that his own home was uncongenial to him." Mrs. Perry had been a Miss Cabot, born and brought up in Boston, but she had stayed a great deal at James Russell Lowell's who had called her his youngest child. Lowell's oldest brother, she said, "was my uncle and I was quite able to distinguish the difference between the warm magical bookish atmosphere of Mr. Lowell's and the cold vacuous intellectuality of Mr. Norton's at Shady Hill where I sometimes had to go to a dull dinner with the Lowell family when I was staying with the Lowells or the poky banality of the James house ruled by Mrs. James where H.J.'s father used to limp in and out and never seemed really to 'belong' to his wife or Miss Walsh, large florid stupid seeming ladies, or to his clever but coldly self-absorbed daughter who was his youngest child." Mrs. Perry said that "Tom of course saw more of the sons than of the women folk and though I know he knew much of what Harry's mother was like he would be too well-bred to tell you! . . . James's mother (even to my own perception as a child) was the very incarnation of *banality* and his aunt Miss Walsh who lived with them not much better. His father always seemed to me genial and delightful (perhaps partly because he had kissed the Blarney stone and always called me 'little sunshine' and talked to me as if I were a grown-up person) but he seemed to me out of place in that stiff stupid house in Cambridge." Boston and Cambridge, on which Henry James had turned his back, were "warm and active and inspiring in those days."

But, to return to Perry himself, he wrote, "Don't be frightened by this sudden rush of letters. I am not a German army and you are not a cathedral. But my note of yesterday was bitten off before I had said some of the things I had on the tip of my pen. . . . I had begun to indulge in Americanisms and that is a habit as bad as talking about one's immortal soul." Speaking of my book on Mark Twain, he could not agree with me about Howells's influence on the author of *Huckleberry Finn*, and later, with more evidence before me, I came around to his opinion. Perry had appeared as "Mr. Arbuton" in Howells's early *A Chance Acquaintance*, and he knew that Howells was not "an authoritative person. . . . He would gently suggest or amiably persuade in minor matters, and often did, but he was never masterful. Nor was Mark Twain an easy victim to the authority of others. No, the trimming, the modifications sprang from his immense love of popularity which was in him from the beginning." Once Perry wrote about the way knowledge creeps into one through the finger-ends while cutting a book: "I have often noticed it. I have cut a book for my wife, she would read me something, always I had seen it. Now, on the rare occasions when I have in my hands a book really worth reading, I take the precaution of holding the book upside down lest I should absorb all the cream from its pages. How the stuff gets to the brain is obscure. It must be something like the process that a Frenchman employs to teach the blind to see with their noses." Perry regretted some of the things he had missed: "When I think that I might have seen Herman Melville, that I refused to go to Buda-Pesth to see Franz Josef crowned King of Hungary, that I never went to Berlioz's concerts, I know that I have accumulated satisfactory grounds for an eternity of anguish." But, although he regretted not having seen Melville, he never read *Moby Dick:* he was always intending to read it but somehow passed it by, like virtually everyone else in his generation. As for Santayana, he wrote to me in 1927, "Wasn't this Melville (I have never read him) the most terrible ranter?" Alone of the older time, the novelist Howells seems to have been fully aware of this great writer.

Perry's letters were collected and edited by Edwin Arlington Robinson, his neighbour in the summer in New Hampshire, where Perry had a farm from which he wrote to me, "I am here in the country bemoaning a bad hay-crop. . . . The farmer is always in trouble, but so is everyone else and will be till we are all become socialists and communists. . . . Then happiness will rule. *Vide* the weekly press" (meaning myself and *The*

Freeman), "excuse my sass." As for the poet Robinson, I met him at about this time at dinner. He broke silence at one moment only. Looking up from his plate, on which his eyes had been steadily fixed, he said to me, "Have you read *Riceyman Steps?*" This was a novel by Arnold Bennett which I had not read, and all I could do was to say so. Then he bowed again over his plate and spoke no more. He recalled the elder Henry James's description of Hawthorne at a dinner in Boston, like "an owl brought blinking into the brilliant daylight and expected to wink and be lively like any Tommy Titmouse or Jenny Wren." Hawthorne too had kept his eyes "buried in his plate."

Actually, Robinson and Hawthorne had much in common, and both were the sort of writers in whom one finds an arcane connection between themselves and the stories that attach to their lives. The real Delia Bacon, about whom Hawthorne wrote in *Our Old Home,* was precisely the sort of person he was always inventing, and how characteristic it was that he should have bought in Concord the house of a man who believed he was never going to die. Real life and fiction seemed to merge in the case of Hawthorne, and this was the case with Robinson also. One day, during a summer, after he died, when I was in Maine, my landlady said to me, "Would you like to see Robinson's birthplace?" She knew the family that had rented it and we drove over to Head Tide. The house was full of coats-of-arms and D.A.R. emblems, which the new tenants had brought in, and on the very spot where Robinson was born, —"just there," the lady of the house remarked,—began a lively talk on the subject of forbears. "Were you one of the Portland Stickneys?" etc. I was distinctly out of it until the lady said to me, "I have a daughter upstairs who would like to meet you." She called up the stairwell, "Patience, come down. There's an author here," whereupon a girl in green pyjamas, obviously dying of consumption, came creeping down the stairs. There was so little left of her that she looked like a painted ghost, and, breathless with excitement, she whispered, for her voice was gone, "Do you know any other authors?" Then it appeared that, lying in bed, she was supporting the family writing articles about old furniture for a Boston paper, while her mother was dreaming of the D.A.R. In the cold fogs from the river, she had scarcely three months to live, and I thought that if ever there was a Robinson story it was this story that was taking place on the very spot where he had been born.

Robinson was a lifelong enemy of the American creed of success, and he had a cult of poverty that appealed to me as a real and vital element of the literary life. AE preached it, and even William James; and I had been much taken in England with the free life of one of my friends who was making a splendid translation of Vasari. He did about a page a day in the English of Vasari's time, and I can remember his beautiful script with the letters interlaced as in some manuscript of the Middle Ages. Walking one summer to Venice, he slept at the Lido, swimming at dawn, and, subsisting on snails and fish which he caught himself, he lived, like Thoreau, on a few pennies a day. Robert Herrick, the novelist, shared, if not this cult, at least a contempt for the American cult of comfort: he broke all the laws of Tawney's "acquisitive society," driven by greed and the lust for power and money. His heroes, whether doctors or scholars, were like Veblen's engineers in their scorn of any but professional aims; and he disliked the business world as much as John Jay Chapman, for whom it was hostile to truth, love and religion. It seemed to Chapman that the Americans had been mentally enfeebled by success, that ours was an unfeeling civilization and that if a man took a stand against any business interest that interest would strike at him on the following day. One could hardly expect a picturesque, pleasing or harmonious social life at a time when trade was dominant as it was at present, and for him the most interesting periods of history were those that had been lighted by spiritual bonfires. He was happy to think of the "martyr age" in which every New England village produced its Bowditch, Emerson, Sumner or Phillips, but he was repelled by the Yankee trader faces, keen-eyed, practical and hard, that looked down in Venice on the shuddering American tourist; for the old Venetian merchants' portraits were so much like them. For the rest, he had often lain awake at night wondering what was the matter with Boston. As much as Robert Herrick, he felt "the bleakness of American life as contrasted with European life," but, touched by its irresistible charm, he also felt, like Herrick, that "Europe is not our way out of the labyrinth." Both these men had first written to me to praise my book on Henry James, a novelist whom Chapman regarded as not worth reading. Savage in his indignation and like Herrick in his point of view, he was a precursor of the critics of the twenties.

I never met John Jay Chapman, though I had fine letters from him, and he wrote to me at the time of my *crise à quarante ans*, "I had the worst sort of breakdown in middle life, fierce and long and baffling, and I feel as if I may know something about the inside of it." When he said he would like to run over to see me, I was obliged to say that I was in a mental hospital and could see no one, and when later I wrote to Barrytown asking if I could see him, I was told that he was on his death-bed. But with Robert Herrick I spent a week at York Harbor in Maine, where he lived during many summers away from his detested Chicago. As an old Cambridge boy, he had been condemned to pass his life in this centre of "conspicuous consumption" and "conspicuous waste," and, reticent, lonely and somewhat embittered in "our least lovely" of civilizations, he had a shrewd eye for human foibles. He told me how, visiting Henry James, he had inadvertently put him to torture on the station platform at Rye, bidding him farewell: he had compelled James to reveal himself in a friend's company beside a shabby third-class compartment. I wondered what Herrick's feeling was about the great lady upon whom he took me to call on a visit to Portsmouth. We had gone first to see the house of Thomas Bailey Aldrich, which had just been fitted up as a period museum, and the great lady remarked how sensible Mrs. Aldrich had been not to pretend that the Aldriches were anybody, or anything more than the family of the captain of a ship. Then she drew up for us a list of the various strata of Portsmouth society, the supreme shipowners, the lesser shipowners, the masters and captains of ships and all the other grades of the local social hierarchy. She might have been the Empress Theodora describing for two travellers the seven concentric circles of Constantinople.

In those days visiting was possible still with servants and roomy old houses like Hamlin Garland's house at Onteora, to which he also invited me, though I could not go there. I think he was mainly interested in me for my books about New England, the old home that his family had left for the West about 1848. He had a feeling of homesickness for New England. This hearty old "son of the Middle Border," about which he had written his best books, said he had not read my *Mark Twain*, but he had been told it was "a brief for the suppressed obscenity" that was "a negligible side of Clemens's genius." Garland hated what he called "this age of nudity and jazz" and he found even in Thomas Hardy's novels "a growing dependence upon fornication," but, vigorous, cheerful and busy himself, he had lost interest in fiction and was more concerned now with the fourth dimension. He was living in Hollywood, writing about our continuing memory after death and about the strange crosses of which a clairvoyant had revealed the burial places in the desert. "I have gone beyond any illusions about my career," he wrote. "Few are interested in me now and no one will be interested in me tomorrow." But he was happy in Hollywood whither he had followed many of his old neighbours of the Middle Border, and he wrote, "I wish you could see our desert flowers this week—miles and miles of lupin, sand-verbena, poppies and the like. Seas of purple and gold! When California sets out to do a thing she does it on a grand scale."

While I saw Hamlin Garland only in New York, I visited Owen Wister twice, once in Rhode Island and once in Philadelphia. When I arrived at the Long House in Bryn Mawr, he was playing on the piano, and I remembered how he had been introduced to Liszt who said he had a remarkable talent for music. Liszt had known Fanny Kemble, Owen Wister's grandmother, of whom there were four or five portraits, one by Sir Thomas Lawrence, in the house, with other portraits of other Kembles and one of Mrs. Siddons, his great-grandfather's sister, over the library mantel. This was the white-haired masculine profile surmounting a dark red velvet dress that Sir Joshua Reynolds had once painted. The house and everything in it seemed a long way from *The Virginian*, the first book, after Bret Harte, of a kind that was frequent later, foreshadowing the generally debased Westerns of the movies. Owen Wister told me that, calling on Henry Adams who was railing at the country, he had broken out, "Oh, I can't see it so grimly," whereupon Adams rose, walked across the room and, laying his hand on Wister's shoulder, said, "Keep the faith!" Again, writing to Mrs. Winthrop Chanler, Wister had said that Edith

Wharton must have a "small cold heart." Mrs. Chanler showed the letter to Mrs. Wharton, then, later, speaking to him, she said, "I've expiated it. I've told you!"

Owen Wister took me to an old-fashioned Sunday dinner at the house of Dr. and Mrs. Middleton Fisher, where two old sisters of Mrs. Fisher were also present that day, a household of octogenarians or even older. They had recently sold their great house and moved into another house that evidently seemed to them a cottage in the slums, although it was a big stone dwelling with gables and verandahs that stood in the middle of several acres of lawn. Great boxes of sculpture, unopened, lay on the grass,—one a recumbent river-god from Rome,—and the walls within were covered with Italian paintings, Claude-like scenes of the Tiber and contadini. They suggested the dream of Arcadia of a hundred years ago. A great family group by Benjamin West ran along the hallway, representing Arthur Middleton, the "signer," with his wife and baby, who lived to become the grandfather of Dr. Fisher, the patriarch of eighty-five or so in a buff worsted waistcoat who carved the roast beef and Yorkshire pudding. The old man's mind was wandering,—he died a week later,—and as he sat in his chair after dinner he picked up old books in Italian and Latin and pushed them over to me, murmuring about them. His wife told me that he read seven languages, and his mind was full of the Middletons and Middleton Place near Charleston: the bookcases and most of the books had been brought from there. He turned over the pages of a book by James Truslow Adams and he said that Adams made mistakes: he spoke of a Richard Middleton,—there was no such name in the family, —he must have been thinking of Russell Middleton, once the president of Charleston College. Their moving had evidently been too much for these frail old souls, who were still living in the world of a far-away past; and I thought of the last scene of *The Cherry Orchard*. One could imagine here too the locked doors, as they faded away, and the old servant left behind, forgotten.

CHAPTER V

"MAKERS AND FINDERS"

I HAD SCARCELY been recalled to life before I remembered a
week I had spent, in 1914, at St. Malo. The guns were just
going off in the first world war; and, held up on my way
home in that little Breton city, I had read Chateaubriand's
Génie du Christianisme. Surrounded as I was by the purple
and gold of the great writer's native town, I was carried
away by the sumptuous prose of the book, everywhere concrete and expressive, and I then conceived of writing a semi-
historical pageant of my own, "creating a usable past," one
of my old phrases. Seventeen years later, at St. Augustine,
in a ramshackle plantation house, under a magnolia tree
covered with blossoms, and with mocking-birds flitting to and
fro, I began to read for *Makers and Finders,* my focus of
interest for twenty years to come. I had already set out to see
the country I was to write about, and, after hundreds of nights
during my illness when I heard the clock strike every hour,
I had formed the habit of rising with the sun. That is to say,
in summer, for on winter mornings I invariably got up at six
or a little before.

My emotional tone had entirely changed from the days
before my breakdown, when I had seen life so largely in

negative terms, when I had been drawn to failures and misfits like Sherwood Anderson's grotesques and Edwin Arlington Robinson's Captain Craig. I had seen Amiel and John Addington Symonds as maladjusted spirits, as I saw in Mark Twain and Henry James victims of their world instead of victors over circumstances. I had had doubts about my treatment of Henry James, regarding whom Owen Wister sent me a letter of Logan Pearsall Smith that corroborated my *Pilgrimage* in certain respects, "Of course to a friend of Henry James's and another expatriated American, the book cannot but be of poignant interest, with its mastery of its subject and of the whole predicament and situation. Having come myself to England much younger than Henry James, and having gone to Oxford, I formed all sorts of friendships and relations. I used to wonder at Henry James's foreign feeling in England, his sense of not being really at home with English people, and I remember his own saying that he felt he understood Americans better and still saw things with American eyes. I suppose I shall have to pay for my expatriation somehow, but I shan't have to pay for it in Henry James's way." But about Mark Twain I could not feel that I had been mistaken, and I was to repeat substantially in *The Times of Melville and Whitman* the thesis of my original book about him. No attempt was really made to reply to the evidence I had assembled. The frustrated writer,—Melville was a type,—had seemed to me characteristic of our still pioneering country, but I had now read Emerson over and over in order to write a biography of him. Besides this "spiritual germ-cell," as AE called him, "of American culture," I had reread thoroughly Thoreau and Whitman; and I had begun to see the figure in the carpet where I had once seen mainly the seamy side. If I did not "reverse" myself, as certain critics said, it is true that something was reversed in me when, besides the visible civilization, I saw the invisible which these great writers had exhibited to me. Lewis Mumford told me later that my changing point of view had been evident in my letters of 1925 when I had been writing the life of Emerson that seemed to me my least successful book. As a sailor in the navy, Lewis had carried Emerson with him, and in *The Golden Day* he had acclaimed the great writers to whom I had done so little justice. Lewis, in fact, was naturalizing in the minds of American readers many artists who had not been regarded as artists, not only the architect Louis Sullivan but Roebling, Eads and Olmsted, creators of new cultural forms in a world of adapters.

This was a time of discovery, or, as Waldo Frank said, of rediscovery, when the expatriate mind was turning homeward, when Parrington was writing his *Main Currents of American Thought* and Carl Sandburg his biography of Lincoln. A hundred years earlier Audubon had discovered the birds of America, George Catlin the American Indians, Asa Gray the plants and John Lloyd Stephens the old Central American peoples, while many minds now were bent on following Stephen Benét's "Westward Star," uncovering the roots of the native American culture. Constance Rourke had undertaken an ample historical account of this, and John Brooks Wheelwright was at work on a history of American architecture for which the notes were "mounting like a sea." So he wrote to me in 1932; but he and Miss Rourke were to die before their work was finished. Harold Stearns came home, after thirteen years in France, to write *America, a Reappraisal*, and Edmund Wilson's *Europe Without Baedeker* expressed a disillusion with the old world that would have been inconceivable twenty years before. Europe was no longer a sanctuary, and John Gould Fletcher wrote to me on his return from England, "To call a thing 'European' now fails to ring a bell in American breasts." He continued, "The list of great European writers seems steadily to grow less," while the growth of American biography and history made America everywhere interesting, so that it seemed possible to live in the remotest corners. "I think Europe is tired out and one cannot expect more from England, France and Italy than they have done. Nobody here sounds new deeps. Of course Europe is a great continent and it will go on emitting sparks of genius like Wells's book in his romance of the 'World Set Free,' but with dimming lustre." So AE said in one of his letters. It was noticeable that the old expatriates Bernard Berenson and Gertrude Stein who had spoken of themselves as "We Europeans" were to call themselves "We Americans" in days to come; and Gertrude Stein said on her return, "So much has happened since I left. Americans are really beginning to use their minds, more now than at any time since the Civil War."

One could scarcely maintain any longer the negative view of the twenties,—of *Civilization in the United States*, for instance,—as one listened to the émigrés who had come from the boiling caldron of Europe, the phrase of George Grosz in his memoirs. One found "universal hatred" there, George Grosz wrote, although it was true that, coming to America, the caricaturist was destroyed in him, for so little here lent itself, he said, to distortion. He could no longer express despair or disillusionment, and the lover of Raphael and Ingres came to the front in him but with far less of the old authority and force. Among other cultural insiders, however, Gaetano Salvemini and G. A. Borgese, who fought with great effect the Fascist Goliath, found themselves productive in a civilization where they had full freedom of expression and action, even if they had to forge for themselves a "new English-speaking subconscious," as another émigré acquaintance said to me. This was a Russian theologian who had been driven to Germany, after the Soviet revolution, and, driven from Germany, after the rise of Hitler, had come to the United States to learn a third language. He had written books in both Russian and German and was attempting to write in English, on the subject of freedom of speech, when he suddenly died.

But the effort to forge for himself a new English-speaking subconscious was a little too much for Borgese, though he wrote his fine book on Fascism in our language. He had hoped to prove that a foreigner could write an idiomatic English poem, and he was obliged to defend with a quotation from Michael Drayton the phrase, in his *Montezuma*, "the jaguars jerked." He meant that the jaguars moved abruptly up and down. But he gave new value to another phrase when he sent me his visiting card inscribed "G. A. Borgese, American Citizen, April 12, 1938." Borgese always called me "Brother," as if I were a fellow-Carbonaro, and he and Salvemini included me, an old lover of Mazzini, in the group that published the manifesto, *The City of Man*. Then there was the tumultuous Ernest Bloch who was living on the coast of Oregon "in silence, with the ocean, woods, clouds, the great spirits of the past" and who told me that one of my books convinced him that he was right in his vision when he composed, in 1926, his symphony "America." I had been introduced to Ernest Bloch, on the street in New York, at the time of his arrival in 1917, and, having heard, in Carnegie Hall, his first grand recital, I was ready to agree with Pablo Casals that he was the greatest composer of our epoch. Now, living, as he wrote, "in a frightful mental solitude, amidst all the fads and false values of our time," it "required an incredible tension to go on," he continued, "and *create*, in spite of all." These émigrés were the most appreciative readers of my historical series, and George Grosz said that he was taking *Makers and Finders* to Germany three or four weeks before he died there.

Of course there were thousands of exiles from Europe, among them Maurice Maeterlinck who spent five years in New York at about this time: often I looked up at the windows of the Hotel Plaza where this great writer of the past was living. Maeterlinck might perhaps have said what the daughter of a great Austrian author wrote in 1941 to me, "Nobody who has not gone through the harrowing experiences of these last years in Europe can appreciate the marvellous sensation of freedom which I found in this country." But I doubt if Maeterlinck had any interest in the country. I only know that he had written well of Emerson, and I am sure that most of the émigrés saw the distinctive American tradition in Jefferson, Thomas Paine, Emerson, Whitman and Lincoln. They expressed, these men, the Pelagian optimism of the doctrine "If I ought, I can," which Pelagius, in the fifth century, carried to Rome, the doctrine that recurred in Emerson's "Self-Reliance" and in most of the peculiarly American thinkers and writers. It had seemed to them that the Augustinian doctrine of total depravity, allowing no scope for the will, destroyed the whole point of human effort, and against the plea of human weakness they were bent on exhibiting the power of human nature.

It seemed to me that this doctrine was operative still in the American mind and that our literature showed it from first to last, while it had to fight now against the dispiriting but fashionable neo-Augustinian obscurantism. What Thoreau called "the low spirits and melancholy forebodings of fallen souls" had been more and more prevalent since the first world war, and these desperate or fatigued hearts were soothed by St. Augustine, whose *Confessions* actually became a best-seller of the time. But Jefferson, Paine, Emerson, Whitman and Lincoln were cited from India to Ireland in appeals from America drunk to America sober, and I had letters from India and saw essays in *The Aryan Path,* referring to Americans, that said, "They have forgotten Emerson and Whitman," writers who were close to the Mahabharata and whose America brought the world together. I had watched Diego Rivera painting in New York his marvellously living heads of Jefferson and all these other worthies in whom he saw the heart of the American tradition. As late as 1959, Kalidas Nag in India said to George Biddle, "India has always revered America for Jefferson and Thomas Paine and Lincoln. Now we sometimes wonder if you have changed as a nation." George had replied, "At times some of us have the same misgivings." It was certainly Jefferson who had given America an import of its own, who had made it not merely a meaningless free-for-all. Sir Herbert Read once said that I could not forgive T. S. Eliot for leaving his country and becoming a British subject. But, with apologies to Sir Herbert Read, this is quite untrue. My objection to Eliot was that he made a popular intellectual cause of attacking what gave America its uniqueness and distinction.

A strong belief in this idea had reconciled me to the vast Philistine waste of an actual country in which twenty thousand persons a year visited the house of Billy the Kid and how many, or how few, visited the house of Hawthorne? Scarcely enough to keep the roof repaired. Americanism had come to mean the opposite of what it had meant once, and the American moral outlook was identified now with the gangster stories or, at best, with technical expertness. So at least George Orwell said in one of his essays. The motto of America was assumed to be "My fist in your face"; and what could one think of a country in which people spent $908 a year for motor cars and only nine dollars for books? But the writers, at least, were always speaking of an unfulfilled promise of which they never quite despaired, and meanwhile our literature had become a world literature, perhaps in default of any other. One sign of this was the deference paid by Yeats, the greatest poet in English of his time, to the two Americans, Eliot and Pound. Was it perhaps true that, as one émigré remarked, "The old countries are dead for many generations"? It was certainly true that two German publishers said to me at an exhibition of their own fine work in printing and format, "Yes, but unfortunately we have nothing to publish." The French, who had once spoken for the world, had little to show now but a few prophets of despair. The Scandinavian countries had no more Nexös or Johannes V. Jensens, no more Knut Hamsuns or Sigrid Undsets; they had only the author of *Barabbas*; and nothing came to us from the Netherlands or from Hungary or Russia. It was plainly a time of exhaustion, at least in northern Europe, and the vacuum was filled by American writers.

Meanwhile, self-confidence in practical affairs had been succeeded by "self-confidence in matters of the mind and taste." So Henry B. Fuller, the old novelist, said in 1925, and he continued, "We are actively interested in ourselves and are actively expressing that interest through the arts—and doing it in our own fashion." The day had passed when American ambassadors went to Buckingham Palace "as fast as their hands and knees could carry them," Mr. Dooley's characterization of Walter H. Page; and American writers had been throwing off their dependence on literary England since Howells promoted the novelists of Russia, Italy and Spain. James Joyce, "the enemy," as John Eglinton called him, "of the whole English literary tradition," was read more in America than in any other country. Besides, a generation had grown up to write that had no associations whatever with England. Yet the past of our literature was little known, partly because Mencken despised the Anglo-Saxon element in it and because Eliot virtually ignored it. Had not James Huneker called "our demigods of plaster and plush, Emerson, Poe, Longfellow, Hawthorne, Lowell, Walt Whitman, the biggest group of self-illuded bores that ever existed"? These influential critics were not interested in the past of a literature of which they were critical leaders; and how many Americans knew their own past as well as the Spaniard who wrote *The Tragic Sense of Life?* Unamuno quoted Channing, Oliver Wendell Holmes and his "favourite American author," Phillips Brooks. "I love the sermons of Phillips Brooks," he said to Bernard Berenson. It seemed to me that this literature and art had by no means been explored, although there were teachers of them in all the universities. There were fifty Americans who were interested in the Western sheriff Wyatt Earp to one who had ever heard of Thomas Cole, the founder of the Hudson River School whose diary and letters would surely reveal one of the most adventurous of artistic lives. Only the other day Herman Melville was drawn out of the shadows, and Emily Dickinson only the day before that, and how many others were there of whom people should all know but of whom biographies had never been written?

There was, for instance, no life of Ernest Fenollosa, the great scholar of the Far East whom the Japanese emperor appointed Commissioner of Fine Arts for the empire and to whom he said once, "You have taught my people to know their own art." I had seen this man from Salem, this graduate of Harvard, described as a "European scholar," and meanwhile I was rebuked for writing about Henry Charles Lea, the historian of the Spanish Inquisition. A well-known professor of American literature asked in a review who this Lea was that one should write about him, although Lea was recognized the world over as the first of all authorities on his subject. To be sure, there existed one life of Lea, but no one had ever written about Alexander Wheelock Thayer who spent his life, as consul at Trieste, collecting the materials for his unsurpassed biography of Beethoven. Then there was Henry Harland, the American founder of *The Yellow Book*, and there was Marion Crawford, the once famous author whose papers and letters were still to be found at Sorrento. There was George Perkins Marsh, the founder of the conservation movement, the ambassador to Italy who died at Vallombrosa and who influenced the forming of the Italian constitution. What great and exciting lives all these had been, virtually uncommemorated by American writers! There was James Jackson Jarves, the early collector of Italian art and a fine writer of art criticism, and there was Hiram Powers, no more a great artist than Joseph Severn, yet English writers had produced two lives of Joseph Severn, while no one had ever written a life of Powers. There was James Huneker, who, although he despised the American past, had done so much to deprovincialize the country, and Frederic E. Church, the painter of Latin American scenes, whose journal and letters were still to be found in an old house overlooking the Hudson. All these names seemed to have been written in water, and it was only the other day that John Lloyd Stephens, the great writer of travels, emerged from the darkness, a man who should be as famous as any of the literary travellers, English or French, whom all the world knows well.

These were a few of the names of men on whom nobody had written at the time when I undertook *Makers and Finders* and who remained to be "discovered" as Henry Adams discovered the scarcely known Yale professor, Willard Gibbs. How many others were there of the sort that other countries evoke, for the sake of the present, from their cultural past? For instance, the Confederate general, David Hunter Strother, the charming old artist and writer who was famous before the Civil War and whose notes, diaries and letters had been preserved, recalling a time when gentlemen drew, naturally and unpretentiously, as they had written sonnets in the time of Shakespeare. But the "teacher critics" set their students to writing one more book on Eliot or Faulkner or Melville or Henry James, the handful of canonical authors who were regarded as Scripture by the orthodoxy that prevailed on almost every campus. While unexplored subjects were lying about in every corner like the relics of Roman cities in Asia Minor, hundreds of students were at work elucidating texts they were not mature enough to make anything out of. We needed free men of letters who could write *con amore*, and not for the sake of academic advancement. English writers did so. Why not ours?

There was no doubt, moreover, that sectional interests prevailed over national interests in our literary purview, that the West distrusted New England and that the South disliked it and would not recognize the merit of its literary past. One of the best critics of the South said that the "slow poison" of New England was at work even at the time of the Revolution, and New England had come to seem a small foreign country in the Western mind, which had risen to literary power,—a country as remote from anything one had to know or understand as Holland or Switzerland or Denmark. It rejected the claims of a region that had produced perhaps two-thirds of the best literary thinking of the country; for could one say less of a little domain in which Bowditch's *Practical Navigator,* Webster's *Dictionary,* Bartlett's *Familiar Quotations* and Bulfinch's *The Age of Fable* were comparative trifles in a brief period that witnessed the appearance of Hawthorne, Emerson, Prescott, Thoreau, Emily Dickinson, Motley, Dana and Parkman, not to speak of Albert Ryder and Winslow Homer? It was part of my purpose to bring the sections together and create a feeling for the nation as a literary whole.

I wrote primarily for the authors of my own time, for I felt sure that a living sense of the tradition behind them could not fail to interest these authors. I mean the national tradition that is, in Walt Whitman's phrase, an "evolutionary outcome" of the world tradition, the part that represents our own peculiar experience and that is properly seen as a gateway to the rest. As for the sense of tradition itself, one could say that in all the arts it "assures the continuity of creation," as Stravinsky put it; and it seemed to me that we could best connect ourselves with the great tradition by way of the tradition that we knew. Or that we *should* know, as one had to say it, for until quite lately we had had no collective memory, no sense of a continuous development in our literature and art. "In America no man and no thing endures for more than a generation," one of our novelists had said a few years before. The American past that Mencken was bent on "liquidating" was mainly a nineteenth-century past, and the nineteenth century was the *bête noire* of the first world-war mind that was determined to "kill" it, as Gertrude Stein remarked. The whole past, not our past alone, vanished with the world wars, and culture, in the nineteenth-century meaning of the word, was largely abandoned during those years. Culture became what one of our humorists called "conversational parsley," and a great aim of writers was to "get rid of the baggage of memory . . . Memory must be killed off," as Henry Miller said. The artists of the nineteen-twenties attacked what they called "the cult of the past," the "decadent past" whose cultural fabric Wyndham Lewis set out to "wreck," and the new generation, growing up with no knowledge of the past, knew and read only a dozen contemporary authors. They grew up "with no cultural background," Katherine Anne Porter said; they "came up . . . were educated, you might say, not at schools at all but by five writers, Henry James, James Joyce, W. B. Yeats, T. S. Eliot and Ezra Pound." A teacher at Smith College told me that in forty years the cultural memory of the students had become a blank: when he first taught there all the students had recognized any allusion to *Jane Eyre, Pendennis* or *The Scarlet Letter*, while a generation later they recognized nothing. America had gained immensely in the space-sense, in its consciousness of the planet, but it had lost almost altogether the time-sense, that is to say, its consciousness of the past.

So naturally the younger writers had little feeling for our tradition; and, as for others, countless Americans of the old stock were growing up without any inherited knowledge of the history of their forbears which the earlier Americans seemed to have had from birth. Meanwhile, millions of foreign-born citizens and children of the foreign-born were unaware that America had a past. Many of these were the "cultural tramps" of whom Ole Rölvaag spoke, the new Americans who had lost their old-world cultural heritage and could

not find another in their new-world setting, and in many
cases they had come from Europe to escape from their own
past: they wished for no past of any sort, only a future. I
believed it was important to show in all its concrete fullness
the largely unexplored range of our cultural tradition; and,
if this appeared to me surprisingly complex and rich, it was
partly because I had come late to the study of it. I had been
repelled by American history because our historians presented
it as almost exclusively military and economic, with scarcely
any reference to literature, science and art. We had little of
the social history that Trevelyan called the "life-blood of
civilization," and did this not, partially at least, explain the
short-range mentality that prevails so generally in this country,
the fact that "we are a nation of sprinters; we almost never
win the distances," as one of my correspondents wrote to me?
Speaking of the theatre, Lee Simonson once remarked, "We
have not learned to buttress the present with the past. In the
interims we have nothing to sustain us. Like youth, we seem
to live on our hopes, and not, like the more mature publics
of European theatres, on our memories, the interest on our
emotional and intellectual investments." Certainly the lack
of a tradition was not responsible for all our ills, but did it
not partly explain the abortive careers of so many of our
writers, and I dare say also of many of our artists? "In Europe
that's never been the case," James Thurber said one day,
speaking of "the curious idea that the writer's inventiveness
and ability will end in his fifties." Was it not true, as Lee
Simonson said, that Europeans lived on their memories, the
interest on their emotional and intellectual investments?
Their past projects itself into their future, and this no doubt
continues to be true at a time when Europe is relatively
sterile.

I could not take for granted any knowledge of most of the writers whom I discussed in my history of the "Tree," the phrase that Debussy used as a general emblem of all his work and that I took for an emblem of tradition. When someone asked Nicholas Murray Butler about the writers of our day, he replied impatiently, "There aren't any," and I, on the contrary, found too many writers in the past, or so several critics pointed out. I was called undiscriminating, too easily pleased, because, without praising them unduly, I spoke of many who showed "the body of the time," its "form and pressure." My critics had not noted the point that Egon Friedell made in his *Cultural History of the Modern Age*: "The standards of cultural history are by no means the same as those of aesthetics. In the latter, a work of art is valued according to its absolute significance; in the former, with regard to its physiognomic character. Seen in this aspect, it may happen that works of eternal significance receive but a casual mention, and those that stand incomparably lower are considered in detail." I could not be said to have ignored the few great American writers, and, if I was accused of mentioning writers whom my critics had never read, I had my own good reasons for doing so. I was obliged to enter the imaginative feeling of a time when Emily Dickinson, visiting Cambridge, felt it was like Westminster Abbey; and, when it seemed to her that a story by Harriet Prescott Spofford was "the only thing I could not have written myself," how could one ignore Harriet Prescott Spofford? Or how could one ignore *The Pearl of Orr's Island* when one realized how it had influenced Sarah Orne Jewett? It is the minor books or writers that body forth a culture, creating the living chain that we call tradition.

In short, I discussed all the writers at a time when critics admitted only a handful as worthy of discussion, my object being, unlike theirs, not, first of all, aesthetic, but, as Egon Friedell calls it, physiognomic. "Not too damned much," Hemingway's phrase, was a motto of a time when nothing was more distrusted than plenitude, the plenitude of the great men of an exuberant past; for instance, the plenitude of Paderewski whom I heard when he was seventy-two and who gave at the end of his recital no less than twelve encores for a handful of admirers gathered about the piano. I broke in this respect an unwritten law of modern critics, as I broke another by dwelling at length, in a planetary atmosphere, on the literary history of a single nation. For, along with the sense of the past, the sense of nationality had also been largely effaced in the expatriate twenties. Nationality was the thing that Ford Madox Ford hated most; and did not the writers who set the tone of our time agree with him in that age of deliberate exiles? No one seemed to distinguish between the two kinds of patriotism, ignoble patriotism and "the noble kind which aims at ends that are worthy of the whole of mankind" (to quote Albert Schweitzer in *The Decay and Restoration of Civilization*). As any hint of the past came to be called "nostalgic," so any hint of nationalism was "chauvinistic"; and, if I was to carry out my plan, I was obliged to incur the hostility of critics.

CHAPTER VI

INFRA-RED INTO ULTRA-VIOLET

O NE EVENING, at the Academy of Arts and Letters, Carl
Sandburg was proposed for membership, and an old white-
bearded poet rose to say that the heavens would fall if we
elected this roughneck from the West. He read aloud a poem
of Carl's about a man shaving in a sleeping-car while he looked
out over the prairie, and he defied us to elect the writer of this
balderdash who had never apparently heard of Poe or Shelley.
I have not reread that poem, which was probably far from
aesthetically nice, for all the word-magic of which this poet is
capable; and I reflected that Carl Sandburg is a bard, like the
popular singers who wandered through Greece, singing the
deeds of gods and heroes. Or he is like the poets of eastern
Europe, as a Polish writer has described them in *The Captive
Mind*. It is the function of these men to speak of subjects
that are of interest to all the people, and they are not expected to be aesthetically nice. In short, they are public poets,
unlike the newspaper poets but equally unlike the cultivated
poets who are fugitives from what they call mass-culture. Carl
was the opposite number of the very different Robert Frost, one
speaking for the East, the other for the West. Both diffused
about them a great air of space and time, as if they had survived
from an unhurried older epoch.

At the office of Harcourt and Brace, the publishers, where I had spent a year, I had edited and named Carl Sandburg's *The Prairie Years,* the first two volumes of his life of Lincoln; and there, as my only other exploit in this world of publishing, I had brought in the three volumes of Parrington's great work. Carl Sandburg's passion for Lincoln safeguarded in the general mind the will to resist authoritarianism, and he was the only man I knew who could use in good faith the much-abused phrase "the American Dream." Michelet said that almost all literary men lack the sense of the people and its sap, and Carl, who cared little for the public, was close to the people in whom the healthy life-blood continues to run. He had a passionate spirit of devoted love and faith in man, and he never forgot that the first cry of a new-born baby everywhere says, "I have come through! I am." In him, at a time when the world seemed moribund to others, all things seemed to be beginning; and, like some old Swedish scald, he appealed to high and low, as the "household poets" appealed in generations past. He was at home all over America, whether in the woods of Michigan or in the little Connecticut village where he once came to visit me: he borrowed a guitar from the doctor there, and, as the evening flowed on, all the village dropped in to see him and hear him perform. He sang, recited and told stories until four in the morning, as he might have done ten centuries ago in Sweden on one of those long winter evenings in the castle halls of the Middle Ages. He had written a preface for Segovia's book, and Segovia had said, when Carl played for him, "Your feengers need dees-ee-pleene," which was no doubt true. No more than his poetry was his music aesthetically nice, but one might have said this of many of Walt Whitman's poems. Carl was a folk-genius and one of the rarest. He told me that when the "new" critics attacked him as a poet, he fell back on being a biographer, and when they attacked him there he fell back on folk-lore. To me he recalled Goethe's phrase, "Little men pay with what they do, big people with what they are."

He was as canny as Robert Frost, and the politician was strong in him. He had been asked to be Henry Wallace's "running mate." He had fellowship with Henry Wallace,—this was his key-word, "I had fellowship with him." He had fellowship also with Adlai Stevenson, who lives, he said, in the future, adding, "There *can* be hope of great days to come, great days possible to men and women of will and vision." He told me that he went back to Pater and his essay on Charles Lamb for style and would still read him three or four more times. Then one day, in what he called our "steamboat house" in Bridgewater, the village to which we moved in later years,—the house that looked like an old Fall River boat,—he told me that he had a story about two birds in a doughnut cage who had eaten their cage and flown away, whereupon, put in another cage, they ate that one more slowly. He had another story about two squirrels who had not been introduced and whose only thought was to collect nuts; then one finally met the other and said, "Anything special?" He called these stories "trifles that maintain my sanity." One day I took him to my neighbour Alexander Calder's house, that cross between Montmartre and *The Peterkin Papers,* where Louisa Calder was reading Emerson's essays, and everything in Sandy's workshop, so full of childlike whimsy, suggested to Carl some word or phrase. It was "a planetarium, an aquarium, a gymnasium," and he called one object "astronomical moment" and another "the independent universe." He called Sandy himself a "maker of silent music." Of one of the "new" critics he said that this writer seemed to be a nice smooth plank lying on the ground, but, if you lifted it up, there was a scurrying of little black not so nice creatures underneath it. Then, saying he had been offered two thousand dollars for writing an advertisement, he spoke of "the ease that flowed through me when I said No." I understood what he meant, for a similar offer had been made to me. I had had several letters from a middle-aged man in Milwaukee who said his only wish was to be a playwright, who had thrown commercial opportunities over his shoulder,—so he wrote,—in order to "pursue the dramatic muse." He was broke, his wife had deserted him, he was in despair and suicidal. Would I help him to get one of his plays produced? Knowing nothing myself about the theatre, I turned the play over to Edward Sheldon, and it was produced for a few days in New York. Then I received another letter from this man whom I had pictured as wasted, hollow-eyed, bleak and dreary. He said he wanted to see me for a particular purpose and would take an afternoon train to Westport. A plump, pink-faced exuberant fellow climbed down to the platform and offered at once to give me a thousand dollars if I would write an advertisement for a famous Milwaukee beer. I would not even have to sign the advertisement. This was the playwright, and he had a large salary as advertising manager of the Milwaukee beer. A similar ease flowed through me when I also said No.

Carl told me this story when we were driving down the Connecticut valley from Dartmouth College. It was a narrow winding road, and when we gave Carl the wheel he began to drive like a man who is drunk or crazy. He had never had such a chance before, he said,—at home he was not permitted to drive at all, and, shouting a new poem that was on his mind, he ricocheted along the road and almost ran into every car that passed us. We were happy to deposit him at last at his brother-in-law Edward Steichen's house, with wide windows overlooking a laurel-bordered pond. There, at Ridgefield, was

Brancusi's golden bird, and there were white-blooming lilies from Africa, masses of tuberous begonias and a drawing by Charles Sheeler in black and white.

Carl Sandburg was the perfect type of the "infra-red" mentality that was giving place in the thirties to the "ultra-violet,"—in the phrase of *The Yogi and the Commissar* of Arthur Koestler,—one of those yea-sayers and lovers of life who were suspected and disliked by the smaller, more intense spirits of the coming generation. He spoke for the generous, expansive note of a time of diastole, when the future still seemed full of promise, while a time of systole had come in when there was "no future any more," in the much-quoted phrase of Gertrude Stein. Carl embodied the prophetic tradition of Jefferson, Emerson, Whitman and Lincoln that persisted, I was convinced, in our collective mind, though all the great causes seemed moribund after the Spanish civil war, with all the great ideas they had expressed. The change in the literary climate was indicated in a dream of which one of my correspondents wrote to me and which I relate in the words of his letter: "I had a dream last spring. I dreamed I was walking on a grassy plain when, above me, two or three hundred feet in the sky, appeared a glass platform. Standing on this platform were three men whom I somehow knew to be Thoreau, Whitman and Emerson. Then there was tossed down to me from one of them a large circular loaf of bread. It landed with a thud squarely at my feet. I picked it up and held it for a moment in my hands. But then some lions appeared and I hurriedly broke up the bread and threw it to them."

This was "a pretty exact picture," my correspondent continued, "of what may be a widespread psychological situation. I love Whitman, Thoreau and Emerson, but I am also afraid of the lions, and I am on the ground with them while Emerson,

Thoreau and Whitman are up in the air." Very exact this picture seemed to me, and interesting; for it exemplified the change in the literary climate that was taking place in the nineteen-thirties. These older writers expressed the prophetic tradition from which we Americans had once derived our nourishment, we who had carried on the nineteenth-century dream of Faust, Brand and Zarathustra, myths that had been forecasts of the future; and the lions now on the ground were the new dominant writers who were antipathetic to their predecessors. These new writers, whether Eliot or Pound or D. H. Lawrence, whether Kafka or Valéry or Auden, were opposed to the "infra-red" note of the past generation. The notion of man's perfectibility in a plastic world had given American writers an impetus and drive to "ameliorate humanity," as Comte put it, and even Frank Norris and Dreiser had not despaired of seeing injustice reduced by human effort. For the rest, the general motto of our art and letters had been Nietzsche's "stimulus to life."

But the ultra-violet state of mind that was taking over the literary scene was based on an eschatological despair of the world, and this was a delayed reaction of the first world war and the exhausted mind of contemporary Europe. The "blood-dimmed tide" of Yeats's phrase had engulfed the spirit of the West, creating a total disbelief in humanity or progress, and the mediæval notion of original sin reappeared to picture men as the predestined victims of their weaknesses and vices. Emerson's faith in self-reliance had sprung from a confidence in human nature that seemed no longer tenable to the younger generation, and Thoreau's demand that the individual should start life all over again struck them as impossibly ironical at this moment. Where Whitman's generous imagination had seen in war-torn Virginia a prodigality of orchards, flowers and fruits, an elastic air, a scenery full of breadth, they could see only the waste land, a sterile and desolate country, a rats' alley full of stony rubbish. As Whitman and Emerson had been impressed by the worth and good sense of the people, the writers of the new time were similarly struck by their lusts, cupidity, violence, sinfulness and evil; and no doubt they expressed the mood of world-war soldiers who had found corruption everywhere they went, in China, Japan, the Philippines, enough to destroy in them their inherited belief in human goodness. Flaubert, the great artist, for whom people in general were fools or knaves and who filled one with a loathing for mankind, became for contemporary writers a patron saint. Writers who disliked their fellow-men had taken over the literary world, and where love had been the dominant note of Romain Rolland, for instance, the note of the new writers was contempt and disgust. They seemed to dislike not only the "mutable rank-scented many" but all the other "hollow men." One felt above everything contempt in the minds of Eliot and T. E. Hulme, and of Joyce, Pound and D. H. Lawrence.

Because they lacked the vision of evil, Whitman and Emerson, according to Yeats, had come to seem superficial, though he might have added that they were not more superficial than the modern writers who lacked the vision of good, the goodness of the unspoiled human nature that Hemingway found in Spanish peasants and Schweitzer and Alan Paton in the African black men. Besides, Whitman found evil enough in *Democratic Vistas* and Emerson in the brutal elements at the core of life, the habits in human beings of the snake and the spider. But writers now were bent on seeing evil and blackness in everything, and they delighted in asserting the imperfectibility of human nature and in saying that man was fated to be barbaric. The denunciation of liberalism, as Julien Benda had pointed out, became virtually obligatory for men of letters, and, while hope was the only four-letter word that was impermissible, the temper of the time brought to light authors of the past who chimed in with the mood of the authors of the present. Lord Acton's constant historical sense of the wickedness of men corroborated Spengler's disbelief in progress, and St. Augustine's view that men have a positive wish to do evil was borne out in Joyce's mediævalism. Yeats was a hater of everything modern, of democracy and science,—he believed in "inequality made law,"—and D. H. Lawrence, who also believed in the divine right of kings, disbelieved in popular education. "Without contraries there is no progression," William Blake said, and even for those who still believed in liberalism and humanism there was something to be gained from this turning of the tide. For them, it inevitably produced new definitions and a cutting down to the bone of their beliefs. Moreover, it produced as well a kind of interiorization that a period of outward expansion had largely ignored. But with Aldous Huxley's *Brave New World* and Orwell's *1984*, all thoughts of the future were virtually blotted out, or all that were not reactionary or nugatory. A future that was only menacing was not to be thought about when people had lost all faith in their power to change it.

My old friend Sir Alfred Zimmern, who was now a Connecticut neighbour, felt outraged by the way in which writers of the time were influenced by the events of the world-war epoch. The wars, from his point of view, were the result of blunders by statesmen at whom the writer ought to look down his nose, and "that writers, of all people, should allow themselves to be turned inside out, or upside down, by headline facts seems to me shocking . . . Having seen some of these politicians close at hand, I protest against their being regarded as makers of history . . . Hitler and Mussolini, Lloyd George and Neville Chamberlain are just butterflies on the wheel . . . It seems to me despicable on the part of a self-respecting writer to allow his whole view of life to be darkened by what are mere incidentals." But whatever it was that caused the wars, their effects were catastrophic, and Eliot's *The Waste Land*, as William Carlos Williams said, "wiped out our world as if an atom bomb had been dropped upon it . . . There was heat in us, a core and a drive that was gathering headway . . . But our work staggered to a halt for a moment under the blast of Eliot's genius . . . All our hilarity ended . . . Our brave sallies into the unknown were turned to dust."

In short, the whole music of our civilization had been reset in a different key just as it had been after the great Lisbon earthquake, that earlier catastrophe of two hundred years ago which so profoundly affected the thinkers of the time. The Lisbon earthquake had put an end to the current optimism, the conviction that "all was for the best in the best of all possible worlds," for it seemed to be incompatible with the previously held belief in a benevolent Providence and the kindness of heaven. Now optimism had vanished once again with the world wars and the mood of the literary world had changed completely. It was divided between the state of mind of Marxists and pessimistic Christians for whom the world consisted only of miserable sinners, and the American tradition went out,— or, rather, went underground,—with all the ideas of the Enlightenment that had given it birth. Mencken had ridiculed this tradition, Eliot rejected it altogether, and the great writers of the twentieth century, as Lionel Trilling said, were opposed to our still innermost liberal convictions. They were all anti-liberal and anti-humanistic, and the literary world seemed to be fixed in the resulting frame of mind as if no other mood were possible for it. Harry Levin's *The Power of Blackness* summed up the dark line that Hawthorne and Melville developed, with a vision of evil like Edgar Allan Poe's, and he described this line as "the true voice of America," embodying the dark wisdom of our deeper minds. But it was the other line of Emerson, Thoreau and Whitman that Tolstoy said inspired him; and one might ask, when has the world connected America with "the power of blackness"? This assumption scarcely went with the oft-quoted remark that Beethoven's Ninth Symphony, affirming the ultimate victory of mankind, was the all-round favourite American composition. Was not Harry Levin forcing the note at a time when thoughts of evil had become an obsession?

In other words, a cultural ice-age took the place of the free-spirited twenties, an age of suspended animation, and writers became like somnolent drivers, yielding to the asphyxiation of the fatalistic fumes that were all about them. Seeking security, their minds went back to the childhood of the race, to the study of myths and origins, to the eternal mother, and one remembered what Gilbert Murray said about the warfare, the prolonged warfare that fell on the world of the Greeks: it brought about a decline of culture, together with a revival of primitive beliefs, the result of a despair of the world and the pressure of forces that men could not control or understand. One found scarcely a trace of the feeling that Alfred North Whitehead expressed, an Englishman who had done much of our thinking for us, "I wish I could convey the sense I have of the infinity of the possibilities that confront humanity,—the limitless variations of choice, the possibility of novel and untried combinations, the happy turns of experiment, the endless horizons opening out." There sounded the old Emersonian note we seemed to have forgotten, although Lewis Mumford continued to sound it in his plucky and ingenious plea for the "renewal of life."

In our singularly disenchanted world, how deep was the fatalism that called any wish to improve things a "God-complex" and that called "do-gooders" the people who cherished this wish. It is true that Aristotle said, when the state is in danger, as our state chronically is,—when the national existence cannot be assured,—attempts to organize the good life must go to the wall. The general mind cannot spend time and thought on any such thing, and no doubt it was natural enough in these conditions that literature should go to the wall also. Perhaps this explained the dehumanization that literature exhibited in our time and the sense that something was very wrong with it. An English critic had written a book that he called *The Withered Branch* to explain what was amiss with the contemporary novel, and another wrote a book that was called *The Broken Cistern* to explain what was amiss with poetry. How many contemporary books spoke of the "end" of something, *The End of Pity, An End to Innocence* and so on, as if they were really suggesting the end of the world, while no one seemed to think of beginnings any longer. "Lie Down in Darkness" was one of the notes of our time, and another was "casting a cold eye," as if all the chances were against one's seeing or finding anyone worthy of attention. A third contemporary note was "A good man is hard to find," which justified our casting a cold eye. The tone of thought of our time appeared to be set by loveless people living in a withered world, harking back to a sterile past and propagating a dislike for life and men. Yet it was only the other day that Mahatma Gandhi said, "Humanity is an ocean. If a few drops of the ocean are dirty, the ocean does not become dirty." Was Metternich wiser in the long run than Grotius, who built his philosophy of international law on a trust in human nature? Was Joseph de Maistre wiser than Mazzini? And did Reinhold Niebuhr, for all his nobility, really know more about mankind than Thomas Jefferson, Confucius or Albert Schweitzer? St. Augustine, the great provincial, knew only the story of the Christian world and the Hebrew patriarchs and kings,—he had no knowledge whatever of the story of the Greeks; and even the Bible had said of man that God was "well pleased with him." What Thomas Jefferson remarked seemed to me reasonable: "I cannot act as if all men were unfaithful because some are so. I would rather be the victim of occasional infidelities than relinquish my general confidence in the honesty of men."

It was not irrelevant to say that the French Revolution, a generation after the Lisbon earthquake, brought back the point of view that the earthquake challenged, a faith in perfectibility and a faith in progress, and while optimism might never return in the old forms the world knew once, it was certain that the mood of despair could not last forever. Either we would vanish altogether in a war of missiles or our mood would ultimately change, though Freud was undoubtedly right in saying that the people of our time "will never again see a joyous world." We know that the Lisbon earthquake was a mere surface wound compared with the universal trauma of the world-war epoch: yet it is certain that without joy life cannot go on indefinitely and that no mood continues in one stay. Diastole must follow systole or the heart stops. So expansion must follow contraction in the general system, and every ending must be followed by the new beginning that no one seemed to contemplate today. When would the new beginning appear? Where would it appear?—if not among the people who have the most vitality, the people of whom one can surely say that they are less depressed than the European peoples by "the man-quake through which we have been passing during the last fifty years." I am quoting Bernard Berenson, who understood very well the sense of futility and weariness in post-war Europe but who believed that Liberalism was bound to reawaken, cast as it was, like Brunhild, under a spell of sleep.

CHAPTER VII

DISAGREEMENTS

I HAD SMALL interest in politics, for I felt with Flaubert that literature was an ocean large enough for me; but I had always been a socialist on the understanding that the levelling was to be not down but up. I was not a socialist in what Wells called "the resentful phase," any more than Norman Thomas or Saint-Simon, who might have been called the founder of the socialist movement, and it seemed to me that socialism, in appealing for the common man, was appealing for his chance to become uncommon. I had in mind the classless world that one saw in *News from Nowhere*, freed from the traits of slavery and the petit-bourgeois; but I believed, like the critic Brownell, in the "aristocratic virtues" that should be "spread in widest commonalty." I felt these virtues should be defended, while one fought to place the masses in a position to share them. Why fight for the sharing of privilege if privilege was not privilege, a benefit, and therefore worth being shared? "Advantages" were obviously advantageous.

Meanwhile, disliking Marxism, I was all for British socialism, unable to see that the British had lost any freedom except the one kind of which we had too much. I mean the economic freedom that enabled us to produce more goods when we had too many goods already, and I hoped to see our standard of living reduced until we were on speaking terms with the rest of a world that was virtually bankrupt. When thinking in duplex apartments was taking the place of the attics in which the thinking of the past had so often occurred, and when the great Republican cry was, not a chicken in every pot, but three cars in every garage, plain living and high thinking seemed to me celestial.

In the "red decade," therefore, with the rise of fascism, I took part in the newly born League of American Writers, an outgrowth of the American Writers' Congress of 1935 that was intended to bring intellectuals together. At that time there was a large market for left-wing publications, and there was a widespread feeling that "something must be started somewhere," as one of my correspondents wrote to me. This person was trying to help a man who was "starting a movement in Tennessee," and he himself presently started a movement to march on Washington, assassinate the President and blow up Congress. But this was the lunatic fringe of a hard core of thinking that appealed especially to writers who were lonely, scattered over the country and irresistibly drawn by the idea of a guild that would bring them together. They were all opposed to the fascism that was at enmity with joy and ready to pool their common interests in the common purpose that was clearly expressed in the "popular front" of the League.

Members of all the political parties were supposed to join in this, defending the democratic cause against the fascists, and they were united on the side of the Loyalists in the Spanish civil war, the particular cause of the moment in all circles. But I noticed at the meetings a large proportion of young men and women who were enthusiastic in promoting the League but who were certainly not writers in any substantial sense of this tortured word. I never knew quite who they were, for they never published anything, and it slowly dawned on me that they were political sitters-in who were taking the League over for the communist party. I did not understand at first how any writer could be enthralled by a party that made mental honesty impossible, but I soon realized why so many were drawn to communism,—they were drawn by the hunger for faith in an irreligious time. A kind of irrational fantasy drew them, and they were drawn also by the sacrifices that communism demanded of the convert. It gave them the feeling of beatitude that religious conversion always gives, even if they had to surrender their spiritual freedom; and this explained their devotion to an underground cause.

One by one the writers who were members of the League resigned, and my own turn came when, as chairman of the Connecticut branch, I was speaking at a mass-meeting in New Haven. Wilbur Cross, the governor of Connecticut, sat on the platform behind me, and suddenly, in the middle of my speech, a note was passed up to me saying, "Announce that Governor Cross has consented to be honorary president." I knew that Governor Cross had consented to nothing of the kind, and I realized that this was merely a ruse to take him by surprise and gain his prestige for the League; so I paid no attention to the note. It was a communist manœuvre, a gambit in the game for power that party members were playing in all the liberal organizations; and I soon disconnected myself from the communistic girls and boys who were destroying the League for all candid writers. I did not foresee at the moment that they were destroying the hope of organizing writers for any liberal action, for any organization that was opposed to what Marx called "the furies of personal interest."

With the collapse of the Loyalists in Spain, all the great causes seemed to be dead; and when Stalin made Hitler his ally the last illusion disappeared that socialism and communism had any real connection. Communism, in fact, did its best to kill democratic socialism, but I would have been ashamed to say that I had not known communists or shared the great hopes of the Russian revolution. I would have been all the more ashamed when men were sent to prison because they refused to betray their friends, as if the only patriotism that was worth anything was a kind that involved dishonour. Meanwhile, the study of Freud and Jung diverted the interest of writers away from political questions into personal questions. In *Travels in Two Democracies*, Edmund Wilson pointed out how unconvincing were the murals in Radio City representing the "upward march of mankind," how pale were the decorative colours and how dim the figures; while the whole idea of progress through collective effort disappeared from the general mind of writers. In many cases they had lost even their feeling for justice; and it was soon not unusual to hear artists say that they had never heard of Sacco and Vanzetti. They had become indifferent to human welfare and they thought it was "impure" to know about such matters. In forty years artists and writers had come full circle; for the reactionism that had given place to progressivism had reversed itself in the years of the wars,—progressivism had given place to reaction. A civilization that was ruled by business was no longer criticized, though it made America hated round the world. We were, in short, a Republican island on a socialistic planet, at odds with all mankind, and our literature seemed passively to accept this fate. For, while writers were not opposed to liberalism, they were no longer actively interested in it. They had become too fatalistic.

One of the results of the change in the literary climate was a series of attacks on me as "the leading patriot of American culture" and as "a narrow and embittered old gentleman with a white moustache" who had stolen his best ideas from Randolph Bourne. This was said in connection with *America's Coming-of-Age*, which I wrote two years before I had heard of Bourne. Then I was a "comrade-in-arms of Bernard De Voto" because I "could see no faults in American life," although I had written of the golden world of writers, so different from the brazen world of every day. Bernard De Voto, moreover, refused to meet me because, as he wrote, he had just attacked me again in certain lectures. "I am a weak vessel," he said, "essentially a genial soul with little backbone," and he was afraid that he would begin to find persuasive reasons why he should suppress or modify his convictions: "Oh, Brooks is a nice chap, he's had as hard a life as the rest of us, in the larger sense we're all working toward the same end, and why make such a fuss?" But it was "important," he concluded, "that the edge of difference ought not to be dulled by any discovery that it was pleasant to spend an evening talking and drinking together." That seemed to me frank and manly, but it did not suggest that I saw eye to eye with Bernard De Voto.

Then at a time when James T. Farrell described me as a "Stalinist,"—he being a Trotskyite himself,—I was called in Russia "a direct agent of Wall Street" and one of my books was banned in communist East Germany. It was said that I had "misused my talents," and a British weekly called me a "critic with skids under" who had lost all my earlier sense of literary values. In point of fact, having written in my youth a kind of social criticism, I had certainly written my best literary criticism in the last volume of *Makers and Finders,* in the chapters on Mencken, Dreiser and Edith Wharton. My historical series itself was called a "family party" and a "voluminous record of filio-pietistic indulgence," reeking of "Yankee racism" and "sentimental nationalism" because I had a mere decent pride in what my own people had accomplished. This work was also called "a special case of merchandizing," although Mrs. Jack Gardner's motto "C'est mon plaisir" had always been mine: I had never had any motive but my own pleasure in writing and I had never thought for a moment of numbers. Does any writer, in fact, ever think of the number of his readers? We write what we write because we are what we are; and then I imagine every writer is surprised to discover that numbers of readers find themselves expressed in what he has written. Another critic condemned my work because he had been unhappily married, and this, he wrote, had "induced a bias of which I hope I am now at least in part free." It was said that "Brooks is not really a critic but a lyric poet *manqué*," and my history was called "anecdotal" when there was not an anecdote in it that was not used for the purpose of exhibiting character. So little did the "new" critics expect to find character in a critical work! One professor found twelve errors in one of my books when six of these errors were his own,—he did not know, for instance, that Melville had two uncles and that I was writing about the one of whom he knew nothing. "The professors certainly have it in for you," Edmund Wilson said to me one day.

I was called a "popularizer," a word that properly means one who makes accessible the discoveries of others, when who had there been for me to popularize? I had done all my own spadework, my history was based on "original sources," and I could feel sure that no one else had gone over my field so thoroughly. Then I had "softened" American literature, ignoring the struggles and triumphs of authors, and I had "hedged" and "weaseled" in revising *The Ordeal of Mark Twain* when I had merely removed exaggerations, the result of the ignorance of youth. I was an "ideological policeman" who, having donned the policeman's blue, had taken up clubs and a gun against all modern authors, attempting to handcuff the writer and blind the witnesses to reality,—I was, in short, a common scold; and a college magazine devoted a whole issue to proving that my work was not worth taking into account. The name of Oliver Allston, suggested by Washington Allston, and incidentally the name of one of my sons, was said to have come from my love of the Puritan qualities of Oliver Cromwell, qualities that my critic described as "all-stone." Above all, I was "nostalgic," a word that re-échoed for twenty years in almost every description of *Makers and Finders,* as if I had longed to live in every moment of a past that I saw through a sort of "amber haze." Anyone who read, for instance, one page of *The Confident Years* could see the absurdity of that.

Every morning, as Zola put it, I was obliged to swallow my toad, and I half wished to reply to my critics with the Arab proverb, "The dogs bark, but the caravan moves on." The caravan certainly moved on, but I could not pretend that I was indifferent to the barking, and I remembered the bitter chagrin of my old professor Irving Babbitt when he was attacked on his appearance in New York. The poet Woodberry had been actually crushed by John Macy's review of his writings in *The Freeman,* and Howells had written to a younger fellow novelist, "You'll find [the critics] can still hurt you long after their power to please you is gone." But I also remembered what Coleridge said about the "petulant sneers" of reviewers and Henry Adams's remark, "You can't kill a critic. Reply is like scratching their match for them." Especially I remembered Turgenev's last word of advice to writers, "Never try to justify yourselves. Carry on your work, and in time everything will come right."

But would it come right? I often wondered. Some of these accusations were true,—I mean some of those about *Oliver*

Allston,—and Lewis Mumford pointed out why I failed to reach the young as I had reached them in my earlier writings. I had not quite understood why the "power of blackness" had taken over the literary world. Then I remembered George Orwell's remark that a writer's tendency, his "purpose," his "message" was always what made him liked or disliked. "The proof of this," Orwell said, "is the extreme difficulty of seeing any literary merit in a book that seriously damages your deepest beliefs." Had not Claudel said of André Gide, who did not share his Catholic philosophy, "I don't see that Gide has any talent at all"? I was disliked because I felt with Crane Brinton that "We Americans are still children of the Enlightenment," a statement with which Herbert J. Muller, Ashley Montagu and Erich Fromm, all good thinkers, agreed. For myself, like most Americans, I still believed in "reason, freedom, human progress, the whole box of tricks belonging to the classistic-humanistic virtue-ideology," as the Jesuit Naptha said in *The Magic Mountain.* I was an infra-red type surviving in an ultra-violet epoch, and those who disliked this tendency ceased to read me.

In short, I was still "middlebrow," retaining the old American faith, at a time when the intellectuals were inveterately highbrow and when I was said by a certain critic to have supported the highbrow once, in *America's Coming-of-Age,* for instance. My critic had forgotten the motto that book bore on its title-page, a quotation from *Timon of Athens,* "The middle of humanity thou never knewest, but the extremity of both ends." I had written for the cultivated, not the "grey-plaster temperaments" with what William James called their "pedantifying ways," and I still believed that Sainte-Beuve was right in saying that "sound criticism has its action only when it is in concert with the public, and almost in collaboration with it." I could not think that the "close" critics who were the highbrow critics, with their class-room studies, were the true guardians of literature, any more than the journalistic followers of Mencken; and it seemed to me that Sainte-Beuve and Hazlitt, Charles Lamb and Macaulay were all, as the highbrows would have put it, middlebrow writers. I agreed with Thornton Wilder, who remarked in *Writers at Work*, "It would be a very wonderful thing if we could see more and more works which close the gulf between highbrows and lowbrows."

As for the time when I wrote *America's Coming-of-Age*, we cast our lines innocently then and caught whatever came out of the great ocean; but that was before the days of the "new" critics and before the days of an avant-garde. Meanwhile, I had a letter from a young writer in the South who said, "To me the most terrifying thing about the mind of the 'new criticism' is its unwillingness to accept any point of view except its own, or any literature except of the elected party liners. It has taken into the universities the very doctrines of exclusiveness and intolerance which have made the world they are attempting to escape." To me it seemed that the highbrow critics had gone up into a stratosphere that left humanity far behind them, and I felt that their only salvation was to descend to the middlebrow level and reëstablish some sort of relation with our common human nature. We needed a Dostoievsky to tell the intellectuals that they must humble themselves, for they were more to blame for the chaos of our literature than the mass-culture they were always deploring. Henry Adams had set the key for the "new" critics when he said that "society contained no hidden qualities that artists could appeal to." But he said also that John La Farge did not agree with him, and John La Farge was an artist as well as a writer. It was the artists and writers who interested me.

Now it was the change in the literary climate, as well as my point of view, that affected the critical fate of my *Makers and Finders*, and Malcolm Cowley explained this very well in a review of one of my later books: "He had spent twenty years in writing *Makers and Finders* and the first two volumes (1936 and 1940) had been received with unqualified, almost universal praise. The last three volumes (1944–52) were praised with reservations or condemned without them, although the volumes were excellent in themselves and completed a useful and impressive project. What had happened was that fashions had changed, that a new group of writers had reached a position of influence and that they did not accept Brooks's project as critical in their own definition of the word; some of them didn't even bother to understand what he was doing. The new critics were not interested in the historical background of a work of art, or in the experiences or character or intentions of the author, or in the social effects of the work, or in the climate of literary opinion at a given period. They called themselves 'ontological,' in the sense that they were interested in the work itself as pure essence or being. They proposed to study its structure and texture, its internal relations, its rhythms and images and symbols, while leaving everything else to the sheer journalists or the mere scholars. Some of their studies proved to be extremely fruitful, as Brooks himself is willing to acknowledge. He quarrels with them partly because they magnify the importance of form at the expense of subject-matter, but chiefly because they refuse to admit that other critical methods are also justified, including his own"; and, Malcolm Cowley continued, " 'How many writers' conferences,' Brooks says, 'how many books and magazines dwell each year, with fanatical concentration, on the "form" of writing, never diverting a moment's thought from the question, How to write well, to the question, How to live well to be a writer.' All his life Brooks has asked that second question, which was central in his biographies of Mark Twain and Henry James. When he did not find the answer there, or found only part of it, the question led him further. He had observed that most American writers failed to develop and mature after a first display of their individual talents. He believed that their failure was largely due to the lack of a continuous literary tradition, something that would support and sustain the individual writer and give his work 'more than an isolated meaning' . . . At the end of his studies he decided 'that, collectively speaking, our writers formed a guild, that they had even worked for a common end—an elevating end and deeply human—and that living writers, aware of this, could never quite feel as they had before, that they were working alone and working in the dark.' "

In *Makers and Finders*, I might add, it was not my view of life that the "grey-plaster temperaments" quarrelled with,—it was rather with my methods and my governing idea; but with *Opinions of Oliver Allston* the case was very different, though the verdict reflected on all my writing. I seemed to have sinned in attacking the writers who controlled the literary mind of the time, and, in fact, I confess my fault in failing to make it clear that I was not attacking their qualities as artists. I had said specifically that in literary capacity and vigour of style, in talent and even in genius, this was "beyond all question one of the brilliant epochs," and what I condemned was what Orwell called the "purpose" and the "message" of the writers, just as the critics united in condemning me. I might say that Archibald MacLeish did the same thing in *The Irresponsibles*, knowing that the writers he attacked were admirable artists. He and I both said what Orwell said in *Inside the Whale*, that many intellectuals allowed themselves "to be swallowed by the whale," remaining passive, not protesting the conditions of a time in which "only anti-humanism, perversity and jeers could thrive," as one of my correspondents wrote to me. Regarding writers,

there are always two points to consider,—the first is their calibre,
the second is their tendency. It is by their calibre that one ranks
them as writers, but critics in general cannot believe that one
appreciates this unless one fully accepts their tendency also.
Yet how can one fully accept the tendency of certain contemporary writers whom one's aesthetic sense most heartily enjoys?
No one doubts Hemingway's calibre, and few can have failed
to enjoy his books; but how can one like his point of view of
the typical American super-male, the redblooded he-man who
despises "sissyness"? Hemingway has taken his point of view
from the bar and the ringside and he has raised it to the level
of literature. It is for just this that his cult-followers admire
him, and it is just this that worries me. As long as this point of
view prevailed on the ringside alone, it did no harm to the things
I care for. But when it received the sanction of art it went far
to destroy the values on which art itself is based. For what does
"sissyness" comprise if not the traits of the sensitive man that
art has hitherto cherished and nourished? As one of the soft-
boiled myself, I cannot like this tendency, and it seems to me
deleterious and regressive.

So, regarding several contemporary writers, I was attacking
their tendency just as Belinski, the Russian critic, attacked the
great Gogol for his newly acquired reactionary views. But to
have attacked in any way idols of the avant-garde was to have
invited the censure of critics who were interested mainly in
their structures and their textures and who so largely ignored
their essential content. How much had gone unsaid when, as
Eliot put it, "The critic must not make judgments of worse or
better. He must simply elucidate," or when, in the phrase of
I. A. Richards, a critic required "the detachment, discrimination,
patience, persistence and sharp cutting edge of a biologist,—
with the underlying assumption that that is all." Did not this

mean dwelling on the mint and cummin to the total neglect of weightier matters? It was the result of following "the letter," as Eliot prescribed, leaving all to the experts and repudiating the public that had always been the final judge. Criticism became an end in itself, an art existing in its own right, and, losing its feeling of responsibility to the public, it expressed all sorts of irresponsible positions. It said, for instance, that Joyce's blindness and Darwin's attacks of vertigo were "symbolic self-punishments for the 'impiety' of their work." It also said that Whitman was not an affirmer of life but a death-worshipping neurotic. These preposterous statements could never have been made if criticism recognized a public that would have brought it to book. In this sense I made war on the so-called teacher-critics, the "professional elects" who denounced what they described as "message-hunting" and "author's-intention-hunting" or any emotional participation in the "subject-experience of a literary work." Through them, to paraphase Whitehead, a good period in art died down into scholasticism and pedantry.

Was it true that I had not caught up with the age I was living in? Or, on the contrary, was it true that I looked to the future, to an age in which life would again have meaning and purpose? If the great European writers of our time were hostile to our beliefs, to our innermost liberal convictions,—feeling with Yeats that "violence and tyranny" were "not necessarily evil" or believing with Lawrence in the "dark forces" that would destroy toleration,—then, however one admired these writers, one had to regard them with a certain scepticism; and I saw that younger writers did not regard them sceptically but swallowed their illiberal ideas with their literary genius. The ideas in question were slowly destroying the resisting power of imaginative minds, stifling their confidence in life and their confidence in men, along with their motive for opposing regimentation. This was the result of not considering subject-matter but passively accepting everything that had a new style; and thus young writers, nominally liberal, were no longer actively so, and they became fatalistic and increasingly sterile. Partly in consequence of this, as a friend in California wrote to me, "The tide of pessimism and cynicism runs so strong that modern life begins to seem a betrayal of humanity." The oxygen for writers had been drawn out of the atmosphere, the result of ignoring the spirit and following the letter. It seemed to me that a new literary epoch was long overdue.

CHAPTER VIII

AT WESTON

WE HAD built a new house at Weston, four miles from Westport, on a high plateau overlooking the Sound. It was a brick house, painted white, with a verandah at each end and in front a broad stone terrace from which on sunny days one saw Long Island twenty miles away. Our clearing of four acres was surrounded by woods, and one day I saw three deer grazing on the apples that lay on the ground under the old orchard. During the first year wild forest birds were all about us, mourning doves, wood thrushes, whippoorwills and hawks that built their nest in a great oak near by; but after the garden was planted the forest birds disappeared and the village birds discovered us. The robins, catbirds and bluebirds had followed us out.

It was 1941. We had disposed of our cottage in Westport and now, disentangled from village affairs, we could live more serenely with our work and with the friends who came to see us. One of these was Victor von Hagen to whom and his wife we lent the house one winter. Victor was writing at the time a life of John Lloyd Stephens, the old explorer and traveller in the Central American jungle, together with a smaller book on the artist Frederick Catherwood, who had gone with him to

97

Guatemala and Yucatan. Stephens had written his classic "incidents of travel" about these regions a hundred years before, and Catherwood, who had studied Piranesi in London and the great ruins of Egypt and Greece, had drawn the splendid illustrations that accompanied the text. Catherwood, an architect in New York, had been forgotten, like Stephens, and Victor reconstructed their lives as one reconstructs, for a museum, a dinosaur from two or three petrified bones. He had unearthed Stephens's letters in a New Jersey farmhouse and he discovered Stephens's unmarked grave in an old cemetery on the east side of New York, where the great traveller had been hastily buried during a cholera epidemic. Victor had been stirred by my account of him in *Makers and Finders,* for Stephens was one of the lost writers whom Melville had seen in his childhood and whom I was bent on resurrecting.

Victor had led an adventurous life. His *métier* was the American tropics, and he had lived all over Latin America and among the primitive tribes on the Amazon river. Well he knew the sleepless nights, the howling sore-ridden dogs and the biting insects in the villages of the Kofanes and Huitotoes. He had not yet undertaken the great exploit of his later years, the rediscovery of the ancient Inca highway, the route of Pizarro in Peru, but he had climbed to the original El Dorado, the Andean lake of Guatemala, and he had scaled the southern Sierra Nevada with its Tibetan-like people and looked into the emerald mines of Muzo. As a naturalist living for two years at the headwaters of the Amazon, he had collected specimens for Mexican museums, and he had taken to the London zoo a live quetzal, the sacred bird of the old Mayans. In fact, he had raised quetzal birds in his camp in the forest of Ecuador. Moreover, he had spent six months on the Galapagos islands, among the great turtles that Captain Cook had found there, and now and then he would disappear into some small island of the West Indies. Victor's book on John Lloyd Stephens was largely written in my study in the house at Weston.

I had had my name taken out of the telephone book, and this was partly because of a convict who had been discharged from Sing Sing and who called me night after night. He said he was a friend of Heywood Broun who had run a free employment bureau for several months during the depression, but the generous Broun to whom I wrote did not know his name and I somehow conceived the morbid notion that the man in question was prowling round the house. But one day came the voice of a man I had known when he was a boy, and I later remembered that this boy, thirty years before, had struck me as coming to no good. There had been something sinister about him that warned me against him,—I had never felt that way about any other boy,—but when he uttered his name on the telephone I had forgotten this and I was glad to do what he asked of me. He was a captain, he said, in the army, and on the train to New York his purse and all his money had been stolen, and would I lend him twenty-five dollars to be given him at the General Delivery window? Never hearing from him again, I remembered the little boy of whom I had had such doubts when he was ten years old. We lived for a while in a movie melodrama with a German cook and her son who turned out to be Nazis. Finally we got them out of the house, after the boy had run away four times looking for other Nazis, threatening to murder village schoolchildren and bragging that he was to be the next Führer. Then he began to have epileptic fits. We found that a charitable society in New York had a long case-history of the two; and they agreed to see that the tragic pair would not put poison in anybody else's soup.

To the Weston house came once William Allen Neilson, the

president of Smith College who had been one of my old professors and who still called me "Boy" when I was sixty. It reminded me of my other professor, Edward Kennard Rand, of whom I had been so fond when I was at Harvard, the great mediævalist and classical scholar who had asked me to call him "Ken," saying, "Age counts for nothing among those who have learned to know life *sub specie aeternitatis.*" I had always thought of that lovable man as many years older than myself, although he was perhaps only twenty years older, and he confirmed my feeling, along with the feeling of both my sons, that teachers of the classics are invariably endearing. I must have written to say how much I had enjoyed his fine book *The Building of Eternal Rome,* and I found he had not regretted giving me the highest mark in his old course on the later Latin poets, although in my final examination I had ignored the questions and filled the bluebook with a comparison of Propertius and Coleridge. He had written to me about a dinner he had had with the Benedictine monks at St. Anselm's Priory in Washington. There had been reading at table, especially from two books, Pope Gregory the Great's account of St. Scholastica in his *Dialogues* and my own *The World of Washington Irving.* He said, "Some have criticized your book as being neither literary criticism nor history. Of course it was not meant to be. Some have felt that Washington Irving comes out rather slimly, but let them look at the title of the book." He felt as I felt about this best of all my books, that it was "really tops."

Two or three times, C. C. Burlingham came to lunch with us in Weston, that wonderful man who lived to be more than a hundred years old and whose birthplace had been my Wall Street suburb. His reading ranged from Agatha Christie to the Book of Job and he had an insatiable interest in his fellow-creatures, while his letters were full of gossip about new poli-

ticians and old men of letters with whom he had been intimately
thrown six decades before. I could never forget the gaiety with
which, when he was both blind and deaf, he let me lead him
around his rooms to look at some of the pictures; and once when
he came to see us in New York he walked away in a rainstorm,
unwilling to hear of a taxi or even an umbrella, although he
was at the time ninety years old. There were several men of
ninety or more whom I knew first or last, all of whom were still
productive and most of whom knew one another as if they had
naturally come together at the apex of their lives. I never met
John Dewey, whose style was a sort of verbal fog and who had
written asking me to go to Mexico with him when he was in-
vestigating the cause of Trotsky; but I liked to think of him
at ninety swimming and working at Key West long after Hemingway had moved to Cuba. At Lee Simonson's house, I had
dined with Edith Hamilton, the nonogenarian rationalist and
the charming scholar who had a great popular success with *The
Greek Way*. Then there was Mark Howe and there was Henry
Dwight Sedgwick, an accomplished man of letters who wrote
in the spirit of Montaigne and produced in the end a formidable
body of work. I saw Sedgwick often before his death at ninety-
five,—he had remarried at the age of ninety,—and he asked me,
when once I returned from Rome, if I knew the Cavallinis in
the church of St. Cecilia in Trastevere. I had to confess that I
had missed these frescoes, recently discovered, that he had
studied in his eighties. Sedgwick had chosen to follow the philosophy of Epicurus whom, with his followers, Dante put in
hell; but he defended the doctrine in *The Art of Happiness*, and
what indeed could be said against the Epicurean virtues, health,
frugality, privacy, culture and friendship? Of Mark Antony
De Wolfe Howe the philosopher Whitehead said the Earth's
first visitors to Mars should be persons likely to make a good

impression, and when he was asked, "Whom would you send?" he replied, "My first choice would be Mark Howe." This friend of many years came once to visit us in the house at Weston. Then I spoke at the ninetieth birthday party of W. E. Burghardt Du Bois, who embarked on a fictional trilogy at eighty-nine and who, with *The Crisis,* had created a Negro intelligentsia that had never existed in America before him. As their interpreter and guide, he had broken with Tuskegee and become a spokesman of the coloured people of the world.

Mr. Burlingham,—"C.C.B."—wrote to me once about an old friend of mine, S. K. Ratcliffe, whom I had first met in London in 1914 and who also came out for a week-end in Weston. "Did you ever know a man with greater zest for information? And his memory, like an elephant's, stored with precise knowledge of men and things and happenings." His wife, Katie, "as gay as a lark and as lively as a gazelle,"—she was then seventy-six,—had "a sense of humour that has been denied S.K., but neither has any aesthetic perceptions. People and books are enough for them." S.K. was visiting C.C.B. and, not waiting for breakfast, he was off to the University Club, where he spent hours writing obituaries of living Americans for the *Manchester Guardian* or the *Glasgow Herald.* Later, rising ninety, he was beset by publishers for the story of his life and miracles, as he put it, but, calling himself the Needy Knife-grinder, he had spent his time writing short articles and long letters and could not get even a small popular book done. Then, all but blind, he said there was nothing in *Back to Methuselah,*—"G.B.S. ought to have known that,"—and "I look at my bookshelves despairingly, knowing that I can have nothing more to do with them." However, at eighty-five, he had still been busy writing articles, reviewing and speaking, and I had never before known an Englishman who had visited and lectured in three quarters of the

United States. Finally, colleges and clubs took the line that speakers from England were not wanted any longer, even speakers like S.K., so unlike the novelists and poets who had patronized the Americans for many years. With their facile generalizations about the United States, these mediocrities, as they often were, had been great successes. While S.K. did not like Dylan Thomas, I liked his poems very much, but I made the mistake of telling Dylan Thomas so, whereupon he said to me, "I suppose you think you know all about me." I should have replied, "I probably know something about the best part of you." But I only thought of that in the middle of the night.

Many years later I went to see S.K. in England, where he was living at Whiteleaf, near Aylesbury, and he showed me beside his cottage there the remains of the road on which Boadicea is supposed to have travelled. He was convinced that George Orwell's *1984* was nearly all wrong as it applied to England, which was "driving forward into uncharted waters," with the danger of a new tyranny ahead. "But however we go, whatever our doom, it will not take the Orwellian shape." With facts mainly in his mind, he was often acute in the matter of style, and he said, "The young who have as yet nothing to say will try larks with initial letters and broken lines. But put them before a situation which they are forced to depict,"—he was speaking of the Spanish civil war,—"and they have no hesitation; they merely do their best to make it real for others." Meanwhile, I was seeing off and on the octogenarian Frank Jewett Mather, the art critic, the professor at Princeton who remembered Irving Babbitt when he was teaching French at Williams College. Babbitt had not yet worked out the doctrine that brought him disciples from Paris to Peking, but he was already regarded as another Dr. Johnson and Mather had climbed Mount Monadnock with him and tramped with him in the Apennines later.

Only in the face of nature had Babbitt relaxed his role of the prophet, for he was keenly sensitive to natural beauty, but, as I had seen at Harvard, he never acquired the composure and detachment of the *hônnete homme* he so greatly admired. Mather felt he owed much to Babbitt for taking art out of a vacuum and relating it to the general concerns of living, saving him from what he called the grim and humourless aesthetic of the New York circle of Kenyon Cox.

But Mather had, in the end, reacted against Babbitt and against the cult of discipline that led Babbitt to use art and literature as means, not as ends. He himself enjoyed the "pleasanter by-products of error" and found his humanist master also grim. Mather was a humanist in the older sense, the kind that is spelled with a small "h," a respector of impulse along with discipline, indulgent to his erring kind, with an educated palate for all the good things of life. He had the zest of the man of letters who was commoner before the "seven devils of war, woe, hatred and murder drove forth the gentle arts from the House of Life,"—as James Huneker once put it; and this led him to revolt against the control of art by "the professors," delightful to them but fatal to the wilding, art. He wrote very finely and freshly on El Greco and Goya, and he was perhaps the first to express a belief with which many have since agreed that Thomas Eakins, Ryder and Winslow Homer were more important painters than Sargent and Whistler; but he would not have argued the point, for Mather was the least contentious of men and one of the most reasonable, humane and open-minded. He was a discriminating, learned and witty writer, all the more to be cherished at a time when the beautiful art of criticism had been so largely changed into a dismal science. He was an old friend of Mahonri Young who often came to see us and with whom at intervals we dined at Ridgefield when he was working on his great monument for Salt Lake City. Ma-honri had managed to get into this not only his grandfather Brigham Young but the whole history of the old plains, and the monument was perhaps more biography and history than sculpture. I liked much better his fifty volumes of sketches of horses, cows, goats, sheep and dogs. Mahonri's father-in-law Alden Weir had once owned the house and farm, and I recognized instantly the truncated willows in the meadows that I had seen in Albert Ryder's pictures. It turned out that Ryder had often visited Weir.

I had written to my classmate Samuel Eliot Morison, whom I had scarcely known in college, to say how much I liked the picture of his countenance in the book that recorded our class twenty-five years later. The book contained two pictures of each member of the class, one taken "now," the other taken "then," and I had been struck by the rarity of the faces that showed a fine development and the commonplace appearance of most of the others. Boys who had been beautiful in college had been coarsened out of all resemblance, while half a dozen, Jack Wheelock, George Biddle, Ned Sheldon and himself, had grown more and more appealing and distinguished. Sam was touched by my letter, and so began for me a friendship with this reincarnation of the fine historians of an earlier Boston. He was a sailor and he took me to task for the "marine solecisms" in my passage on Dana's *Two Years Before the Mast*. I had used the word "cheerily" when, he said, "cheerly" was "the right, the male, the vigorous and the seamanlike word," but it finally appeared that I had followed another edition in which the word was printed as I had spelled it. He later wrote that the sail from Boston to Trinidad was lovelier than he had ever imagined it could be, with effects of light and shade, stars, great golden trade-wind clouds and rainbows arching showers that blotted out whole valleys. He was much taken with a novel of Marion Crawford's that showed a thorough knowledge of the technique of sailing. This was after Sam had written the life of Columbus that had led him to sail the Atlantic to the coast of Spain.

In college, Sam had known George Biddle, whom I saw constantly during these years and after, George with his look of an officer of the Civil War who remained as hardy as a Mohawk. His air was lean and soldierly, he was all decision and command, and he would walk barefoot for miles on burning asphalt, really unaware of any discomfort. He loved to play on his flute eighteenth-century music, a "sort of alcohol rub-down," as he called it. George was always going away to the South Seas, to India, Roumania, Japan, Israel, the West Indies; he spent two or three years in Tahiti, he went skiing in the Dolomites, he lived in southern Italy and southern California, and he was impressed by the Negroes of Martinique, Guadelupe and Haiti, a "slice of Africa in an eighteenth-century world." In Brazil he was sent north by the Ministry of Education, and there he made hundreds of sketches of the Recife carnival and the round-ups of the vaquero country. In India he followed Vinobaji for two days during which he might have been following Mohammed, with old women kissing the dust at his feet, with roses strewn in his path and with camels, buffaloes and paint-smeared holy men. As a craftsman he was always experimenting with mural painting or ironwork, mosaics, ceramics and lithographs, among them the fine bookplate of death on a white horse, the symbol of a mind that was haunted by the sadness of the time.

Meanwhile, I continued to see much of Bruce Rogers, whom I had met many years before when *The Seven Arts* was just appearing. That was during a summer at Peconic, Long Island, where he seemed to spend most of his time carving a ship's model, for no one ever saw him seriously working. He would sometimes sketch with apparent casualness on the back of an envelope an italicized N or a capital R, and one did not perceive that under a mask he was working with intensity and that his appearance of idleness was a sort of pose. Later I thought of him when I happened on Reynolds's praise of Rubens for seeming to make a plaything of his art. It was "the common coquetry of authors and artists," Reynolds said, "to be supposed to do what excites the admiration of others with the greatest ease and indifference, and almost without knowing what they are about. If what surprises you costs them nothing, the wonder is so much increased." To be done well a work must seem to have been done easily: that might have been the motto of this "tramp printer," as he called himself.

After that summer, Bruce Rogers continued to send me at Christmas one of his slender publications, Thoreau's *Night and Moonlight* or *The Centaur* with the errata slip that made this a famous folio in American printing. When I saw one of these advertised later in a rare-book catalogue for something more than three hundred dollars, I recognized Bruce Rogers' style of understatement in describing as Christmas cards these lovely brochures. He had gone to England as a sort of partner of Emery Walker, the former associate of William Morris on the Kelmscott Press, and I wrote to him asking for a few suggestions for improving the format of *The Seven Arts*, which seemed to me generally awkward and ugly. He replied with a long letter saying that the magazine was "nearly all wrong in every typographical detail." We had chosen the worst type possible, the initials were set incorrectly, with too much white space around them, the margins were almost the worst feature and the whole magazine was printed the wrong way of the grain of the paper. When we made a few changes at once he wrote, "You now have the distinction, I believe, of being the only magazine whose initials fit"; but the advice came too late, for *The Seven Arts* died three or four months later. This great typothete, as some-one called him, this prematurely old master, was the opposite number to Stieglitz, the old master of photography, and he was the remote successor of Caxton, Aldus and Benjamin Franklin, who had also called himself a printer. He cared above all for readability. "The most beautiful types," he said, "are the easiest to read"; but he was capable of remarkable nuances. He instructed a compositor to insert uneven thin spaces between certain diamond-shaped units in order to avoid a rigidity that seemed geometric, and he made a Q by cutting off an italic capital T and soldering it to the base of an O at the proper angle. He liked the Italian motto, "Trifles make perfection, but perfection is no trifle."

This learned and whimsical man seemed almost infantile at times in his liking for the most bathetic and execrable puns or word-plays on "fine BRinting" and "Scotch and Bodoni." He designed an ampersand and sent all over the country for specimens of sand-paper, so that he could print his ampersand on amper-sand-paper. He belonged to the world of typophiles that almost rivalled heraldry in its complex emblems and devices; and, for the rest, he had a love of water-mills to which he was constantly referring. His attachment to these water-mills might also have explained his love of Cotman and the English water-colour painters. He had made himself fine water-colour scenes of Naushon island, the Bahamas and England, pictures of Hastings, the Cotswolds and Cambridge where he was for a while the chief book-designer of the Cambridge University press. He had been designing title-pages in the eighteen-eighties at the moment when William Morris was planning the Kelmscott Press, and he presently designed the Oxford Lectern Bible. In the meantime he had a great liking for sailing ships and carved for a Danish square-rigger a figurehead of Joseph Conrad. Alan Villiers told me later that this had been bought by an American collector. For a number of years Bruce made summer trips up the Baltic on grain-barges or Finnish windjammers, and he often stayed in Copenhagen, finding the people there even more sympathetic than the English.

Reading *The Seven Pillars of Wisdom* in 1927, it had occurred to Bruce that T. E. Lawrence was the man to translate the Odyssey anew. He had long wished to print the Odyssey in a style fitting its splendour as a story, and he felt that Lawrence, a man of action who could write swift and graphic English, could make Homer live again. Four years later he was sitting with Lawrence, at Southampton, on the recreation pier, discussing the final points of the translation in which Lawrence had tried to avoid "passenger words" and retain "only words," he said, that "worked." Lawrence won his heart by saying, apropos of his Centaur type, "What a splendid Y, the most difficult letter of the alphabet"; and Lawrence had taken up printing himself, set up a small hand-press and printed his book on the air-force that was called *The Mint*. Coming to England, Bruce Rogers would send a message to Lawrence from the ship, and Lawrence would meet the ship in one of his speed-boats and take him for a trial run down Southampton Water. Bruce Rogers, on his way back to New York, would always stop for a day or two to see Lawrence, and they spent their evenings in a public bar with the proofs spread out on one of the tap-room tables. They talked about ships, the "Joseph Conrad" and the speed-boats that Lawrence was building for the Royal Air Force. About this time I made a translation of some essays of André Gide. I admired these essays greatly, and, having worked over the translation, I obtained Gide's permission to publish it. But I had only one copy of it and the fine printer, who was having a nervous breakdown, lost this copy.

I used to go sailing with Bruce Rogers on the catboat which he kept near by on Candlewood Lake, and later, when I had moved closer to New Fairfield, I saw more of him in his October House. It was ever so charming with its pink brick front and brownish grey pilasters, built, I think, during the Revolution; it stood on a high knoll with a view of the lakes at front and rear and with three kinds of grapes in the arbours. He showed me the little attic room, with a plain cot, in which he slept among old clothes and trunks, with a wildcat from Maine on the floor beside him; and he read me letters from T. E. Lawrence whose Odyssey he had promised to print at the Oxford Press where he had been book-designer. He was planning to give to his own university, Purdue in Indiana, a complete collection of his publications; and he showed me also his first edition of Webster's Dictionary, 1828, which he called one of the finest pieces ever done in America. By that time he was a very old man who had just finished his edition of Dante and who was at work on the *Canterbury Tales;* and, fascinated by the early English authors backward from Chaucer to Beowulf, he asked me where he could find the original Robin Hood ballads. Then he showed me the new terrace and the goldfish pool that he had built, the pool into which he fell one November day and died of pneumonia a few days later.

CHAPTER IX

CATASTROPHE

In the Weston house, my wife died one August afternoon,— we had just come back from California,—and for six months after that I felt like a man who is drowning and who does not know which way to turn. I lived during those months in a nightmarish dream, and even now I feel about my marriage as Thomas Merton feels about his vocation, I was "happy in a way that does not want to talk." My wife had felt there was a collective life to which she was contributing, and, with her mystical belief in the human race and its upward climb, she had scarcely for a moment relaxed her gaiety and courage. It seemed to me, after thirty-five years with her, that life had been taken out of my hands and that I was cast adrift on a desperate sea. Only my work saved me from foundering in it.

I then discovered that strange separation of faculties of which the novelist Howells had written "by which the mind toils on in a sort of ironical indifference" to the part that suffers; and, having reached the middle of *The Times of Melville and Whitman*, I was carried on by its momentum. I felt as James Thurber says he feels, "if I couldn't write I couldn't live," together with the corollary of this remark, I could live if I could write. I was obliged to write in order to keep up my tone, for when I was not writing I was out of focus and felt not only disintegrated but somehow degraded. I believed, when I was writing a book, that I was on trial for my life, but when I was not writing I was semi-idiotic, my mind wandered, empty and aimless, and I went through all sorts of meaningless motions and ended the day in a state of self-disgust. Absorbed in my world of the imagination, I felt vexed and hapless whenever the intrusion of the real world jolted me out, yet when I had finished a book I had an obsessive conviction that I would never be able to write another. Moreover, it seemed to be impossible to print correctly. I read the proofs of at least one of my books five times and found two more mistakes on the fifth reading. But writing had always been my secret asylum when I felt ill at ease in life, and all had been well with me when I thought of my work. I was rather like the mad woman in the "house of mystery" at San José, who had built eight hundred rooms in that wooden Vatican. She felt she was going to live as long as she continued to build.

For twenty years I had been reading seven or eight hours a day, and I read the whole body of each writer's work, the poor and bad books along with the rest. I was saturated in my literary history with the period I was writing about so that I often felt I was living in it, and my books were intended to be read as if they were novels; for my treatment of a given author was shredded through the chapters to fit the whole figure into the stream of the epoch. I wrote a page a day, beginning each morning by rewriting the work of the day before, and I no more wished for a holiday than Matisse who said, "It has never amused me to amuse myself." Meanwhile, I sold the house, stored away my possessions and moved to an apartment in New York. The house was bought by John Hersey fourteen years later.

Not long before this catastrophe, my old friend Paul Rosen-feld died. Almost his last act had been to come to the hospital with a bouquet of rare flowers for my wife, and he promised to return two days later with *Tom Jones* for her to read, but he had a heart attack in a moving-picture theatre. Paul said that what others called his generosity was merely his inevitable thanks to the artists who had made the world a luminous place for him, and I could believe what a friend told me Paul had said to her at a time when a third person had hurt her, "Go out and do the nicest thing you can think of for someone else. That will restore the balance in the universe." The wisdom of William James had come to Paul naturally, for he had grown up with the expansive feelings of the earlier years of the century and scarcely felt at home in a time of reaction. He shared the prophetic beliefs of the old circle of *The Seven Arts* and of those whom he called the "great old Europeans with their feeling of a world full of glorious possibilities and of human beings potentially noble"; and after his death he inspired a follower with a devotion like his own to edit a collection of essays about him. Jerome Mellquist could not rest until he knew Paul would be remembered: he wrote seven hundred letters and he travelled for fifteen months all over the country in order to round up contributions to his *Paul Rosenfeld, Voyager in the Arts*. It was a story of devotion quite unrewarded, and it reminded me of the zeal of the little doctor who appeared at my house, at the time of my breakdown, and offered to cure me. He had read my books, and, hearing of my illness, he had come out to Westport to see me; and he wanted to give up his practice, take a room in the village and devote all his time to getting me well.

No one had cared more for Paul than Alyse Gregory and Llewelyn Powys, who had often walked over from Norwalk in the twenties to call upon us, but Llewelyn had died in 1939 and Alyse was living in England, near Dorchester, at Chydyok, on the southern downs. She had written to me from Davos Platz when Llewelyn was too ill to read or talk, and when she had got up in the darkness at five and had seen the little squares of light appearing, one by one, in the cabins of the peasants. The great sad sanitariums were already a blaze of light after those long hours of waiting. Now on the English coast, where Llewelyn was buried under a great stone shaft, she looked out on fields of ripening barley and bare wild downs and sheep dogs racing in the wind and rounding up the sheep. She watched the swallows feeding their young on the branches of a cherry tree and the blackbirds flying away with a bright red cherry in their yellow beaks. Then, where the grocer drove up only once a year, she toiled, with her milk and provisions, up and down the valleys, living in a Jacobean cottage as the Brontës had lived on their Yorkshire moor and running down a steep slope to greet me. For years later I went to see her there.

Alyse had been in charge of *The Dial* when Paul was a contributor. He had written his *Musical Chronicle* month by month at a time when I first met Newton Arvin who came to my office at *The Freeman* and sat and talked with me on the rim of the tub. For we had taken an old apartment that was not yet made over and the bathroom was the only corner for conversation. It seemed to me that Newton Arvin, that quiet man with a violent mind, would gladly have stood against a wall and faced a fusillade for his convictions. At that time his convictions were on the far left, farther even than my own, but later, when he modified them, he did not go back on them; he never became a reactionary, like so many others. "All of us," he wrote to me, "who took that great bumpy detour of Marxism can very justly be accused of making smooth the way for the college of cardinals that came after us," those who rode into power on the authoritarianism that had first appeared as a doctrine of the left. Waldo Frank still remained of that persuasion, more or less, like Charlie Chaplin who spoke at a dinner that was given for Waldo on his return from a long South American journey. The great-hearted Reinhold Niebuhr was the chairman at that dinner. Waldo, who had lectured in Argentina, Uruguay and Chile, had been beaten in Buenos Aires by fascist storm troopers. He had spoken a language that was quite unlike the language spoken by the business promoters who "treated us as if we were Indians," a Latin American writer said, "and our language a dialect of Quechuan"; he knew the religion of the Latin Americans, their dances and their art, and he conveyed in *America Hispana* a feeling of the tropical cultures that John Lloyd Stephens had written about and that Victor von Hagen recalled in many of his books.

At that dinner I had sat beside Charlie Chaplin, who told me about his recent visit to Japan. He had been carried away by the Japanese theatre. After the dinner he gave a party in a private room, and, pretending that he was a pigeon on the eaves of the Plaza Hotel, he ran about the table fluttering and cooing, making love to a lady pigeon and keeping it up till midnight with a nervous energy that never for a moment slackened. It was like Lee Simonson's energy when he was not demagnetized in one of his recurrent attacks of depression. Lee had designed two ballets for Mordkin, a setting for a condensed Swan Lake and a gay Viennese scene for some waltzes of Strauss, the Johann Strauss whom I had seen as a boy in Vienna, in the very year in which he died. That was in the spring of 1899 and Strauss was conducting his own orchestra there.

Lee Simonson had been at Harvard with my old triumvirate of friends, Edward Sheldon, Maxwell Perkins and John Hall

Wheelock, the first of whom died just before my wife and the second about a year later. Ned Sheldon had been immobilized for nearly thirty years; he could not lift a finger from the bed where he lay; moreover, for ten years he had been blind. No doctor had been able to halt his arthritis, and he could not turn his head, resting on a pillow. Yet, gay as he was and apparently serene, his laughter filled the living-room, dispelling all feeling of compassion for him. He never spoke of his illness or referred to it in any way, and he maintained with his nurses a sort of rigid discipline that kept any suggestion of pity from breaking through. His eyes were bandaged with a narrow black silk mask, and, fully dressed, with a coverlet and a canopy towering over him, he had received visitors all day in his big blue room. The room was always full of flowers and a multitude of books that were read to him, often at night. He read many books on the Civil War, and on a table near his bed was a photograph of his hero, Robert E. Lee. The Confederate side in the war appealed to him deeply.

Towards the end he spoke only in a whisper; his vocal cords were giving out, and he had a thrombosis of the heart just in time, one felt, to save him from a total eclipse of the Not-me. He had usually written or telegraphed whenever I had seen him, and, after the news came that he had died in the night, I received a posthumous message from him. He sent his love and wished that we were having a quiet Sunday, for he knew that my wife was very ill. A few weeks earlier he had written, after we had dined with him, at the little table drawn up beside the bed, "I spent far too much time on Russia, but I suppose the subject is on people's minds these days and I had been listening to the UN meeting for six hours." He was breathlessly interested in the war and well-informed about it, yet he kept up the humorous mood that he had maintained for so many years and sent me a comic letter on his sixtieth birthday. He pretended to look down on me for being still only fifty-nine, and he wrote to me about the pigeons that lived on his penthouse roof and that he called Mr. and Mrs. Homer. They had "two babies of their own, the first brood this year. All this reminds me that life goes on serenely, regardless of wars." He had been, during all these years, an oracle for Broadway, though his life in the theatre was long past and it was many years since his had been the most conspicuous name among American playwrights. Before he became blind there had been a stage near his bed and many plays were tried out within his range of vision. There Geraldine Farrar sang for him, Ruth Draper recited to him, Ethel Barrymore acted for him and Heifetz played for him. "Of course," Heifetz said, "I shall never play in Carnegie Hall as I have played for you today." Once I had lunched there with Ethel Barrymore and, a few years later, when I had made a speech at the Academy and Ethel Barrymore was in the audience, I met her afterwards in the crowded corridor. She said to me, "I'll bet you don't know who I am." Her face was as familiar to me as any face on a postage-stamp, but in the excitement of the moment I had lost all presence of mind and I could not attach a name to this presence in the crowd.

There had been several years before Ned was taken ill when I had seen little of him, for I knew nothing about the stage where he was the white-headed boy on the most intimate terms with half the Broadway celebrities. Among these was Mrs. Fiske who had played in *Salvation Nell*, "the most daring play," one critic said, "that New York has ever seen"; and there was Margaret Anglin who accepted two of his plays, "as yet unwritten," he said to me, "and only in scenario-sketch form." William Faversham had leased a theatre in New York and wanted a play for his next season, and so it went with dozens of people of the stage to a few of whom he introduced me. Then had come the great days when *Romance* had one of the longest runs in the history of the theatre, when it was played in Norway and Sweden, Egypt, India, Australia and Africa and the French Academy took the unheard-of step of inviting Doris Keane to bring it to Paris. A member of the Academy said it was "pure enchantment," and two theatres in Moscow presented it simultaneously with Maxim Gorky's wife in the title-role. At about that time Ned had rented a palace in Venice where John Barrymore lived for a while with him, and he and Doris spent days in New York searching the pet-shops for a monkey that was small and friendly enough to be easily managed. In England he had met J. M. Barrie of whom he wrote to me that he was "such a queer shy little Scotchman with eyes just like Mrs. Fiske's, except that they were a man's eyes." There he became intimate with Somerset Maugham, and he is supposed to have suggested the writing of Maugham's best novel, *Of Human Bondage.* It was based on his early life as a medical student, and Ned thought that in writing it Maugham could overcome the embarrassment that was caused by a defect in speech. Maugham stuttered and this handicap appeared in the novel as a club-foot. Well I remembered the day when, in London, Ned took me to lunch at Somerset Maugham's. That must have been in 1913. Maugham was living in Mayfair, in an elegant little eighteenth-century house, and it comes back to me that there was a bottle of hock on the table and that Maugham was wearing a black velvet jacket. Over the mantel in the dining-room hung a portrait of Billie Burke, who was playing in his *Mrs. Dot,* and, looking up at the portrait, Maugham said, "That is the lady who has made my fortune."

Several years before that, Ned wrote from Cambridge, "Last night we saw *The Great Divide* for the second time. A jammed house, Mr. Copeland was there. We dined first at the Epicure in Boston under a sort of wiry grape-arbour, a dollar table-d'hôte, not a bit bad." Then I remembered him in his apartment in Gramercy Park with brilliantly coloured macaws for decoration, and his delight in the bawdy came back to me, reading an old letter, when he spoke of a Long Island military camp in the first world war. A hackman, asked if the local girls weren't crazy about the soldiers, answered, "Crazy? Gee, the hospitals is full." Later came the letters from the Los Angeles hospital where, walking eight steps in four minutes, with the aid of two nurses, he had felt "as proud as if I had had twins." In his blindness he had developed a sort of second sight and he would guess the height of some new visitor from the position of his voice, so I was startled when he asked "What does he look like?" referring to an English visitor who left as I arrived one evening. He was ruthless in refusing to meet anyone with whom he could not readily communicate. Ellen Glasgow, who admired heroism of any kind, would have been glad to come to his apartment. I was going to arrange this meeting but Ned said No. Ellen Glasgow was very deaf, and Ned felt he could not whisper into the ear-machine that she managed with such triumphant skill.

Ned, who never mentioned Doris Keane or any subject that concerned himself, had once believed that he could stand up to anything, but he came to feel the need of the religion that he never quite accepted. Yet the instinct of religion was very strong and deep in him, and so was the feeling that led him to say to one of his friends, "You must forgive yourself, too. That is the hardest thing of all." It reminded me of Theodore Dreiser who had gone through life bowed down with a sense of guilt for the way he had lived. I dined once with Arthur Davison Ficke at Ridgely Torrence's in Morton Street, and Ficke had been visiting Dreiser at Mount Kisco. Out for a walk in the afternoon, Dreiser was so silent that Ficke said, "Theodore, is there something you want to tell me? You know it's sometimes a good thing to get worries off your mind." Dreiser turned to him and said with a look of bottomless woe, "Everything I have ever done in my life has been wrong," whereupon Ficke said, "Why, Theodore, don't you think there are times when a man should forgive himself for his own sins?" Dreiser ran off a hundred feet as if he had been stung, then, turning round, with tears pouring down his cheek, he said, "Great God, Ficke, that's the most wonderful thing I ever heard;" and every hour or so for the next two days he repeated, "A man should forgive himself for his own sins." Ficke told me this and I was struck by his own great gallantry; for at that moment he was dying of cancer of the throat, yet, entirely ignoring himself and his troubles and his unrecognized work, he insisted on talking about me. However, I knew that inwardly Ficke felt bitterly about the way his writing had been disregarded.

While Ned lay immobile there, the old romantic theatre gave place to the new realistic mood, and it was symbolic of this change that Eugene O'Neill took over Ned's apartment after he died. Ned had read Thomas Wolfe but he could not believe in Wolfe as a novelist. He had written to me, "The complete imprisonment within his own ego, the distorted way in which he sees other people, the lack of any form, architecture or development (which keeps the book perfectly static), all these things bother me," in spite of "some fine pages of rhapsody which suggest the lyric poet." But my ancient friend Maxwell Perkins said that working with Thomas Wolfe had been the foremost interest of his life. Every night, for many months, Max would go back to Scribner's, after a busy day there, and work till eleven with Wolfe revising his writing, cutting out sometimes wonderful scenes in order that the story should be unfolded entirely through the boy's memories and senses. One night they had walked all round Central Park while Max told Tom about a novel he had thought of: it was the story of a young man who goes in search of a father, the very story that Tom Wolfe had been destined to write. Max became his father and confessor. Tom turned to Max to escape from his doubts about himself, and Max would listen for hours while he poured out the story of his difficulties. I had scarcely known of this till I dined once at Max's house on the night when his first grandchild was born. Just before nine o'clock Max got up and left us. He was going back to the office to work with Wolfe. Not long before that, a Harvard instructor, a friend of Wolfe, had been found dead in Westport under a syringa bush. His body was discovered in the cemetery down the street from us, a few hundred yards away. Kenneth Raisbeck was a character in one of Wolfe's novels, and the first selectman of Westport called on me that morning to ask if I knew anything about him. His car had stood all night, with the lights on, directly in front of our house. Was it a case of murder? Raisbeck had been strangled, as I remember, with a wire cord about his neck.

Max had felt in college a wish to be a novelist, and he had turned his energy and will into this vicarious task of "trying to hang onto the fin of a plunging whale." For so Tom Wolfe, writing as usual about himself, referred to Max as an editor and a reviser of other men's-work; and, if I am not mistaken, Max was the first editor who had ever performed this function. Formerly there had been copy-readers and editors only of magazines, but editors of books were, I suppose, unheard of; writers had submitted manuscripts that publishers took or sent back, but I had never heard of an author who expected a publisher to do a good part of his work for him. Max was perhaps the first, as by common consent he was the best, the editor of Scott Fitzgerald, Hemingway and others, always eager to take on some new novelist or some new writer of short stories. I remember how pleased he was when I called him on the telephone to ask if he would like to publish Sherwood Anderson. Liveright had failed and Sherwood was anxious to make another connection. Max broke all records in his effort to get books right, and how many things he did for authors apart, moreover, from their books, dining in their houses in order to work with them later and sending them veterinarians to care for their dogs and cats. Nor could anyone have been more fertile in suggestions. He suggested titles for books or that someone should write reminiscences or "invent twenty-five crimes,"—this to a writer of mystery-stories,—or that a man who had never seen a war should write a tour of the battlefields, taken in company with an old soldier with whom he disputed about them. He wrote to Hemingway wishing he could go, with Fitzgerald and himself, on a tour of the Virginia battlefields. Suggesting a life of Jeb Stuart to one who presently wrote the book, Max was intensely interested in the Civil War himself, and I think that, like Ned Sheldon, he was chiefly interested in the Confederate side. Tolstoy's *War and Peace* was always his favourite novel, the dimensions of which seemed to grow larger every time he read it. He said, "Any book that has in it a journey during which the plot develops has a strong element of interest," and with his delight in river trips he wrote from the White River in Missouri about a week he spent there shooting ducks with Hemingway, "We saw a good many of the river people living in houseboats that were just like those Mark Twain told about. We heard a most terrific racket around a curve, and then there came a regular old-time Mississippi steamboat with two funnels, side by side, pouring out wood smoke. To a Vermont Yankee it was like going back eighty or ninety years and coming into Mark Twain's world." To Edward Bok he said, "Your books run the danger of giving the impression that you overvalue material success." Max even suggested to Winston Churchill, when he came into Scribner's once,—he seemed to be "much more like an American than an Englishman,"—that he should write the history of the English-speaking peoples which Churchill actually wrote a few years later.

If Max was to be remembered many years after he died,— remembered far better than most of the authors he worked for, —it was largely because of his sympathetic understanding and because of the standard he maintained. Perhaps he remembered Goethe's saying about the importance of being always in touch with masterpieces, "so that the creative spirit may be maintained at its height"; for he could only think of revising a book "in terms of some classic that one measured everything of that kind against. If it is a book about a prostitute, it has to be thought of in terms of Moll Flanders." He was always referring to Defoe's *Memoirs of a Cavalier* or Clarendon's *History of the Rebellion* or Boswell's *Life of Johnson* or Spengler's "incredibly interesting" *Decline of the West*. He was certain that the great books stand between the precious and the trashy and speak to the literate and the masses alike. "The great books reach both," he said; and, feeling that few of the great writers had had a formal education, he objected to the way literature and writing were taught in colleges, "It results in one's getting into the habit of seeing everything through a kind of film of past literature, and not seeing things directly with one's own senses." In this he disagreed with the "new" critics. He suggested to one writer a book on the Civil War with the contrast in his mind of Luther and Erasmus, the "man of cool intelligence" and the "impetuous and intense one . . . you should read all their correspondence." He himself stood with Erasmus while he had to deal with "Luthers," if one may so describe Tom Wolfe, Hemingway and Scott Fitzgerald, all impetuous and intense and, as he said of Tom Wolfe, turbulent half-archangels who were half-rascals. Wolfe and Fitzgerald had died some years before, and I believe he thought Hemingway had nothing more to say, so, when his time came, I wondered whether he had really wished to live any longer. Max had been a man in the grand style who was exceedingly attractive to every artist.

As for "that most courteous soul on earth," as Mrs. Patrick Campbell, in a letter to Ned, called our immutable friend John Hall Wheelock, he had written at least two or three poems that were destined to endure when the whole works of many other poets were forgotten. For few had produced any poems that could be compared with *The Lion House, September by the Sea* and *Noon: Amagansett Beach.* I was to walk with Jack, for many years to come, along the great beach at East Hampton with the pedantic little sandpipers, intent on the prey cast up by the waves, and looking out

> On the pale meadows of ocean, on the barren fields and bare,
> That the sea-bird wanders, that the sea-wind wanders.

He wrote to me of the moonlight there raining down over the unearthly country while the dunes resounded to the drowsy music of crickets and cicadas. Jack had found Tom Wolfe tiring and oppressive at Scribner's, although also at times most engaging, but he had appeared in one of Wolfe's novels and in James Jones's *Some Came Running* as a curiously idealized good and learned professor. Then, like George Herbert, who had lost the muse in his youth, he found himself, after so many deaths, living and versing again. Retiring from an active life of publishing, he wrote finer poems than ever, among them

The Gardener, about his father, full of a deep ancestral piety. Then there was the *House at Bonac, Reflections at Seventy* and *A Walk With the Wind*,—

> Waters by heaven rimmed,
> Beaches where as a boy
> I strode, as eager-limbed
> Today as then—O joy,
> Still with me, still undimmed,—

poems more profound in feeling, and certainly more his own, than anything he had written in earlier days. Seventy years of the great beach and the old house at East Hampton had gone into the making of these moving vestiges of John Hall Wheelock's later life and thought.

CHAPTER X

A NEW LIFE

JACK WHEELOCK had known my wife when they were young
at East Hampton, and it was in his New York apartment that
I met my second wife, Gladys Rice, the daughter of Mark
Twain's doctor. Growing up in Irving Place, a few yards from
Gramercy Park, which she described enchantingly in a book
about her childhood, she had written her school compositions in
the bay-window of her family's house, with one eye on the rear
of the Players Club next door. Her father had attended Edwin
Booth on his death-bed there, and she could imagine the company of actors who were gathered in the club, talking about the
theatre and the plays of the moment. She had been married first
in Boston, where she had spent fifteen years and where three of
her four children were still living. There Sargent had drawn a
portrait of her and she had played in a string quartette and
practised with Felix Winternitz, her old teacher. She had been
David Mannes's earliest pupil in New York, and she had had
a full social life in Washington and Paris, where Henry Adams,
of whom she was the last adoptive niece, had read to her from
the unpublished *Mont-Saint-Michel and Chartres*. But of her
one might have said what Bernard Berenson's secretary said to
me of his old master, that, wonderful to relate, he could be so
much of the world yet not be worldly in any sense at all.

Universally sympathetic, imaginative, gay, and almost of my own age, she was called "Gladys" virtually at sight by both young and old, even by children. Busy with her Stradivarius, she played with Allen Tate, whom I regarded as an enemy when I first met him,—for I identified him with the "new" critics,—but whom I ended by acclaiming when I read *The Fathers*, his extraordinary novel of the South in the Civil War. Seldom had I been so impressed by any novel and my uneasy friendship with this fine poet and subtle critic was presently established on a solid basis. I liked to hear Allen and Gladys fervently scratching their way through Haydn and Mozart's duets for two violins,—occasionally joined by George Biddle with his flute,—or through Couperin or Purcell's "Golden Sonata," and I remember Allen saying of my "Coterie Literature" in *Oliver Allston*, "If only that chapter had been left out, how much happier we should all have been!" Sometimes we visited the Tates' rooms in Perry Street with the coal grate, the mahogany heirlooms and the ancestral portraits. During that first winter, Gladys and I went the round of concerts in various churches and museums, concerts of religious music from the court of Louis XIV, motets of Lalande, oratorios of Bach and Handel; or we heard Szigeti playing a Bach concerto and Suzanne Bloch with her virginals and lutes played by Pre-Raphaelite ladies in velvet à la Giorgione. Often Gladys practised Bach sonatas for violin alone. Larry Adler performed for us at our first Christmas party, and later we heard him in Carnegie Hall, which he filled all by himself, playing with his harmonica Mozart and jazz.

We went to many picture shows, Picasso at the Modern Museum, and especially the Metropolitan with all its glories, where I liked best the widespread canvases of Titian, Tintoretto, Veronese and Gladys the small delicately perfect Italians and Dutchmen. She was drawn to the pictures of roses and grapes of the early eighteenth century and the miniature mountains and streams in the backgrounds of the primitives, or a profile painted by Cranach. One day James T. Farrell came to lunch at our apartment. He had attacked me the year before, hitting rather below the belt, but he said to me that day, "I believe you are on the side of the artist." Farrell was writing twelve hours a day, but, an Irishman with a prehensile appetite for learning, he was studying at night at Columbia mediæval philosophy and Freud. Of course he had been trained in Roman Catholic logic. With Sinclair Lewis and Lewis Mumford, to whom he was grossly unfair, he was capable of savage indignation, and I admired him rather for his power than for his direction, although he had become a consistent democratic socialist. Unlike so many others, he was not fatalistic, but I felt that too often he "said everything," which Voltaire called the secret of being a bore.

In the summer we returned to Martha's Vineyard, where I had a cabin for writing in, and where we saw much of Lillian Hellman who, during a picnic on a beach, read us two acts of her play, *The Autumn Garden*. The gaunt shy Dashiell Hammett, who had made an art of the mystery-story, was present on that evening and many others, the man of whom André Gide rashly said that his prose was the best written in America today. Gladys, always active, had gone in for "remedial reading," charmingly responsive to the unfortunate boys whose lives were sometimes wrecked by their inability to read. Direct and compassionate, she conjured out of them all sorts of unsuspected powers, for she was passionately interested in the possibilities of growth that every human being carries within him. The only people she could not abide were the spineless people who did not know when they were being pushed around and who never dreamed of pushing back. Meanwhile, she had learned to like

the ways of an almost servantless world, and she who had once
had nine servants found that the pleasure of doing for oneself
outweighed the expenditure of time and effort.

But, much as we enjoyed New York and the resources of
the great town,—the glass-engravers, the shops devoted to old
china, the museum of Mexican objects that we found on one of
the rear lofts of an office building,—we tired of the plethora of
things where too much was going on, too many telephone calls,
too many invitations; and there were the eternal cocktail glasses
and half-smoked cigarettes that spoke of the last unwelcome
party. If we were to miss the concerts and the art museums,
think of what we missed by not spending our lives in Paris or
London! The quiet of a country village looked very good to us,
so, turning to Connecticut again, we spent a year in Cornwall
and then bought a house in Bridgewater, a few miles south. It
was on the village green, facing the two churches, and, with its
great copper beech, its magnolias in full bloom, its huge
rhododendrons and white birches, it seemed to bring back the
peace of fifty years ago. With its big circular verandah and
shut-in garden, and with chairs set about under the trees, it
suggested many a Sargent water-colour. We introduced ourselves to the postmaster in the store, for we did not know a soul
when we settled in the village, but Gladys was soon playing her
violin in one of the churches across the way, an obbligato of
César Franck or a Vivaldi andante.

It appeared presently that in all the villages roundabout
there were old friends living whom we saw often,—in Sherman,
Woodbury, Brookfield and New Milford. Peter Blume, the
Mantegna of our day, spent two or three years painting a picture, but every one of these, "The Eternal City" or "Tasso's
Oak," was an event of the year when it was finally shown. We
watched these pictures growing in all their stages. Malcolm

Cowley, whose only rival as a reviewer of novels was our other good friend Maxwell Geismar, knew all the birds that visited the Sherman valley, the acorn woodpecker, the sickle-billed thrasher and the three varieties of towhee he found in California. Malcolm had written in *Exiles' Return* the classic story of the expatriates of the nineteen-twenties. The Francis Hacketts were at Newtown, in their Danish house, so clean that no devils could ever enter in; and there lived Louis Untermeyer and Henry Schnakenberg, with his Americana and his great fern alley. Maxwell Geismar, perceptive and acute, often drove up from Harrison, and William McFee and Matthew Josephson lived near us too. The Alexander Calders, when they were not in France, were at Roxbury, five miles away. We saw Sandy once in Rome where, on Good Friday, in Saint Anastasia's church in the via Babuino, surrounded with pious old women, rapt, on their knees, I felt a bunny-hug and suddenly, behind us, there was our irrepressible Connecticut neighbour. He was exhibiting his work in the Obolisco gallery, and he was pursued in the streets by youthful Italian adorers who were taking coloured photographs of him. In our rooms at the Academy, he came to tea one afternoon when Mario Praz was also there,— the critic whom we had previously seen in the Villa Guilia,— and when Sandy left, after carrying on in his usual way, Mario Praz exclaimed, "I am glad to have met Alexander *Korda!*"

Another of our neighbours was William M. Ivins, retired from the Metropolitan Museum, who lived in his old house at Hotchkissville, a museum in itself of rare books and works of art, among them a unique series of woodcuts by Titian. There Bill fashioned the quill pens and manufactured the black ink with which he composed his witty letters. He raised the finest peonies there, and, a sceptic, in his blue work-shirt, a contemporary Diogenes, he did his best *not* to find an honest man.

Occasionally, a quasi-hermit, he plopped about New York, dropping, he said, hayseed with every step in shops and streets, but usually, letting the dust accumulate about him, he stayed indoors and went on with his reading. He had picked up Bayle's Dictionary, the first edition, in French, and he amused himself with the two big volumes, unearthing meanwhile a long run of eighteenth-century writing and finding that he could still wallow in Voltaire. Bill had written, among other books, *How Prints Look,* and he wrote there in the country his study of Vesalius, with the famous anatomical woodcuts. It was certainly true that Bill Ivins could easily have created a vogue in the realm in which he reigned. As curator of black and white art, he had only to mention a name, and repeat it three or four times at cocktail parties, to establish a cult for this name in a few months; for every print-dealer in New York would at once place examples in his window. Just so, the classic Mrs. Astor, by dropping a new name two or three times, created, I suppose, social reputations.

The Wheelocks came out to see us, and Peyton Rous, their brother-in-law, who gave his name to the Rous sarcoma, spent a week-end with us every year. This heather-green-clad scientist, with his eager curiosity, who seemed to have come out of a novel by H. G. Wells, would scramble through the wet woods, with his vasculum swung over his shoulder, spying among the fallen leaves a pipsissewa or a veronica, a bit of grey moss or a partridge berry. Then, once a year or so, the tough-minded little South African Scotsman, Alan Paton, dropped in between Kent and Yale, the author of *Cry, the Beloved Country,* whom we came to love and who was always within a hair's-breadth of a South African prison. The Zimmerns, Sir Alfred and Lucie, came over from Springfield or Hartford, with their never-failing vision of human progress, their faith in the future and their religion of hope, where Lucie, who was the daughter of a French Calvinist pastor, conducted a class for taxi-drivers. She said that her general theme was "driving through life," and I liked the story about the little French village where her family had spent vacations away from Paris. When the local priest died, the whole village appealed to her Protestant father,—until the bishop opposed it,—to be their new priest.

Twice my brother-in-law, Frank Stimson, came up from Tahiti, where he had been living since 1912, and he worked in our house twelve hours a day with his multi-lingual type-writer on his dictionary of the Tuamotuan language. Our house was always flooded with the shells that his daughter sent us, the mother-of-pearl that was used as a lure for tuna and bonito fish and others that were iridescent, green or rose. From West-port came Hamilton Basso, and his Toto, our dear friends, who lived on the edge of a forest, overlooking a stream,—Ham, shrewd, witty and all-observant, who might have been a natu-ralist, as aware as Uncle Remus of the ways of animals and birds. For him, as a novelist, the story in a novel was like the backbone in a human being. Riding with the cowhands in Arizona, he delighted in his escape from the "genteel wilder-ness" and the smooth people at home. Coming from New Orleans, he had left the South in order to bring up his son where he would never hear the word "nigger"; yet, in revolt against the South, he was bound up with it,—he had never made a clean break with the world of his childhood. How well he understood its past one could see in *The Light Infantry Ball*, in which realism was mingled with the actual romance of the old South, so unlike the mythology of the pre-Civil war time with its "soft dream of vanished glories." Ham shared Thomas Wolfe's dissent from the writers of *I'll Take My Stand* with their fictitious chivalry and ideals of honour. An engaging writer of travels, too, he had a way of going off to Finland, or to Denmark, Brazil or Samoa.

It often made me happy to think of the advantages that were connected with a writer's life, especially the people it brought one in touch with; and, when our friends died, there were the younger writers who, in a sense, were contemporaries also. For, among writers and artists, there are no ages, and the world of imaginative minds is self-renewing. Once, for the winter months, we went to Cambridge, near that special social enclave that is Boston, where Hans Zinsser, my old friend at the Harvard School of Medicine, had once urged me to go and live. But I was afraid it would be too pleasant, in that all-cultivated world, and that I might be killed by so much kindness. We spent winters in New York, once below Washington Square, a region of old brick houses reminiscent of Dublin, and I wrote there by a window overlooking a garden in a square near the house where my father was born a hundred years ago. We saw something of Thornton Wilder, John Dos Passos, E. E. Cummings, Stephen Vincent Benét and Edward Hopper, who complained that he was given credit only for painting lighthouses and that people did not seem to have looked at the rest of his work. Edward Hopper's banal scenes, observed under a magic light, were, I thought, pictorial equivalents of Theodore Dreiser, and his wife told me that he had read my *New England: Indian Summer* while he was painting his "Route 6 Through East Ham" on Cape Cod. My book, she said, "went right into that canvas." One day I fell in with Lin Yutang and asked him if he did not feel like a ghost after a morning or a day of writing; for the long abstraction from everyday affairs made me feel curiously wan, etiolated, ashy. Yes! Lin Yutang said, he himself felt just so until he rejoined his solid Chinese wife. The courtly Glenway Wescott, who admired Thornton Wilder and whose own life was a work of art, a believer in clarity and brevity, catholic in taste, had an eager and discriminating interest in younger writers. With his finely finished work, he loved literary politics, and he was, he said, much less a writer than a talker. My wife gave E. E. Cummings, in his rooms in Patchen Place, a much desired lesson in callisthenics, lying outstretched on the floor, with Cummings beside her, while she laughingly exercised the muscles of her back.

In a time of "private" poetry, it struck me that Stephen Vincent Benét exemplified, like Frost and Sandburg, "public speech," so that, with his feeling for what he invoked as the American Muse, he became a sort of national poet laureate. But his work was overshadowed by John Crowe Ransom's fashionable doctrine of poetry no longer written by patriots or prophets, a poetry that Ransom said had gladly lost its public support and solicited only a "small company of adept readers." This was an American form of the French Symbolist doctrine that made poetry a private concern of the poets, and it put an end to Benét's vogue with the critics. But, a child of three generations of West Point men, Benét had been rooted in the history of the country, and he had an astonishing talent for capturing local atmospheres with a special feeling for the long afternoons and the slow rivers of the South. He was a voice of the people, like the household poets of old or like the folk-writers Lindsay, Sandburg and Masters whose reputations had had to struggle against the cosmopolitan aestheticism that had been coming in for a generation. He had the art of making a real folk-legend,— *Johnny Pye and the Fool-Killer, The Devil and Daniel Webster,*—in which inconvenient realities were simplified away, so that these tales had the air of coming out of a timeless

past. I saw Stephen Benét fairly often, and he told me that
his Webster had been drawn from *The Flowering of New
England*.

In these later days, "Marse" John Dos Passos was also
creating a new sense of the American past,—of the "head and
heart" of Jefferson and "the ground we stand on,"—when this
half-Marylander had reverted to his mother's plantation world
and had left behind the radicalism of his second period. For
his *U.S.A.* had succeeded the aestheticism of his first period
in the days of *One Man's Initiation* and *Streets of Night*,
and it seemed to me that few things were more interesting
than the development of this remarkable writer. An inter-
viewer had come to see me in the middle forties who had
just been to Provincetown; there he had interviewed John
Dos Passos who was surrounded, he said, with the old Tory
novels of Sir Walter Scott. I could see there the tendency
that in fact soon declared itself, for Scott, the arch-conserva-
tive, had been a favourite of the old Southerners, and Dos
Passos could not have been drawn to him if he had not had
leanings in the conservative direction. I could see in advance
there the apparent reversal of his point of view, although,
as a matter of fact, Jefferson would have shared his feeling
about people who were ruined by "the big money." Jefferson
would have agreed with Dos Passos's attitude towards a world
in which only social revolutionaries were worthy of respect,
with the confusion of the melting-pot, together with the
wrongness and baseness of the capitalistic system in its hour
of triumph. Meanwhile, this inventor of new technical devices
that made him famous around the world had developed a
real affection for Portuguese-speaking Brazil, where he had
spoken, like his Portuguese grandfather, the language of the

new writers. He even described himself as "a relapsed Portuguese."

Dos Passos was a world-traveller, in Russia, Mexico, the Near East, like so many other writers of our time,—Vincent Sheean, Edmund Wilson, Hamilton Basso,—all of whom were unlike the globe-trotters of former times who had been merely sight-seers and lovers of sensation. The new travellers were eager students in a world that was becoming "one," and Thornton Wilder, for instance, had known the globe literally from China to Peru, the setting of his well-known early story. Wilder's feeling for national temperaments was one of the striking results of his really universal culture. He had known James Joyce, he had fraternized with Camus and Sartre, the writers who made "a vigour and almost a gaiety," as he wrote to me, "out of an accepted despair" that was certainly tonic. He had toured, for the government, Colombia and Ecuador, he took part in the Goethe celebration at Aspen, with Schweitzer and Ortega y Gasset, borne up and along by Goethe, "deep without strain, homely without smallness and all as strong and fortifying as our Alpine torrents." There, he said, "scores of students had hitch-hiked thousands of miles, earning their living by dishwashing or building a near-by air-port." Thornton had lived fully in the age of Spengler, then of Proust, then of Kafka, and, reading Kierkegaard and Lope de Vega, he was looking forward to an old age that was going, he was convinced, to be "buoyantly happy. . . . I am so happy in the fifties that I wish to incorporate into them the inestimable benefits of the sixties, the seventies and the eighties—the permissible selfishness of the aged. . . . I am going to defend myself by calling in the names of Li Po, Anacreon, Sophocles and Justice Holmes,"—all this to explain why he would not serve on committees or waste time reading books by the younger generation. Objecting to what he called the "cold cream portrait painters," he said that an academy does not begin to be useful to society until it has passed its first hundred years; but he had a fine feeling for the French Academy and the glorious *éloges* that Marmontel and Condorcet had delivered there. No one in our day had done more beautiful work than the author of *Heaven's My Destination*, with his power of creating new forms in every fresh romance or play. "There is no arrogance like modesty," he said to my wife one day, apropos of her husband's autobiographical writings.

CHAPTER XI

IMPRESSIONS OF IRELAND

IN THE spring of 1951, I went to Ireland with my wife. After I had got there, I thought of all sorts of reasons why I had originally wished to go there,—for one, that I wanted the greatest possible contrast to the United States after twenty-five years of unbroken immersion in my own country. I hoped to see America from the outside again, as I saw it when I wrote *The Wine of the Puritans* in 1908 and *America's Coming-of-Age* six years later, both books written in England. Then I wished to see it from the most dissimilar intellectual climate in which I could breathe and speak the language.

I hoped to see "characters" in Ireland such as we had once had here, the queer old maids and other odd fish I used to know as a boy, so many of them abolished by psychoanalysis or sent to sanitariums in our streamlined civilization. I hoped to find people better "integrated" than with us, because less modern, and voices with a ring of assurance like those of the old American types whom Fenimore Cooper and Washington Irving described, the "frank sound-hearted sailor" and the "honest soldier," people who lived close to the elements and were brought up in religion and the study of the classics. I suspected that Americans had lived so long the business life, with stocks, paper securities and the like, that they could not any longer see it in its concrete realities as people do in the so-called "backward" countries,—like Ireland, mediæval, Catholic, reactionary, small. I remembered what Gertrude Stein said about Americans, "They have no close contact with the earth such as most Europeans have. Their materialism is not the materialism of existence, of possession, it is the materialism of action and abstraction." I felt with Sherwood Anderson that Americans were at second remove from the soil, bread, fields, stones lying in fields, from the lives of the old artisans and farmers who tasted and felt things through their fingers. Only in Charleston could one have called business the "antique furniture department," Douglas Hyde's name for it in Dublin. At home people talked about health, food, sex, radio, television. What a blessing to get away from advertisements of perfumes! If I saw in Dublin the magazine *Life,* I would say, That is a civilization I don't want to belong to.

Finally, I felt with Thomas Mann that, as time moves faster and faster with every year of our life, travelling is the best way to curb it. "We are aware that the intercalation of periods of change and novelty is the only means by which we can refresh our sense of time, strengthen, retard and rejuvenate it, and therewith renew our perception of life itself. This is the secret of the healing power of change and incident." Older people travel to recover the slow pace of youth.

S.S. *Britannic, April 26th*

Left the ship at Cobh, 8 A.M., on a tender. Fair, warmish spring day. Cobh very like a Mediterranean town, French or Italian,—how surprising. A line of multicoloured stucco house-fronts, blue, pink, yellow, green, facing the harbour. A huge granite Pugin-Gothic cathedral rises over house-tops.

Inactive streets, a few housewives out for marketing, a few priests sauntering about, milk-carts with big containers and dray-horses, shops deserted. A general Sunday air on this Thursday morning. No American electricity in the air, scarcely any pulse, no sounds but those of cart-wheels and horses, with chimes from the cathedral (St. Colman's). Civility and even sweetness in voices and manners, but the ordinary Irish people seem curiously without style in contrast to the English with their soldierly bearing, form in manner and feeling for pageantry in their dress.

At 11:15 we take the train for Cork, changing there for the afternoon train for Dublin. Five hours' journey, first-class carriage rather dirty. Lunch in restaurant car, crude crockery, soup like a watery brown gravy, good stewed meat with tasteless peas and carrots and ready-made jelly. Altogether an "institution" lunch. Swift smooth-running little train with frequent long stops. Runs all afternoon through green farming country. Spring ploughing in fields, wild flowers everywhere, primroses, yellow gorse, small English daisies growing among dandelions. In cottages that we pass wallflowers on all sides, an air of neatness in small houses. The country like a garden, as in England. In towns (Thurles, Charleville, Portarlington, etc.) much grey granite, modern Gothic churches. Passed perhaps two dozen ruined mediæval castles, really only for-tified or castellated dwellings with no architectural preten-sions. History in towns largely ecclesiastical, with memories of old local wars. We passed near Limerick and Kilkenny but not through them and just missed seeing the Rock of Cashel. Scores of miles of lovely quiet pastoral landscape, cows not too plump and sheep unshorn, narrow roads lined with cottages, rivers, the Lea and Blackwater, all agricultural, not a factory chimney anywhere, no smoke, noise or dirt. As we approach

Dublin the stations are finer architecturally, like small Tudor manor-houses. Ruined castles continue to crop up in the fields. Signs of racing at Kildare. Landscape suggests the blue-grass region of Kentucky.

Arrive at Dublin 5:30, sunny late afternoon. An improvised taxi with a smiling chauffeur takes us through miles of streets. He points out the sights, pleased by our exclamations of interest in them. Bicycles everywhere. Young men and women cycling home from work. (Later I saw bicycles banked by the hundred in O'Connell Street, checked for the day for two-pence, under guard.) A great quiet old-fashioned provincial town, in some ways like New York when my father was born there, though of course New York was mean, architecturally speaking. It had little to compare with the great scattered Georgian monuments of Dublin.

The Shelbourne Hotel also like a New York hotel of the 1870's,—the Buckingham, for one, as I remember it,—the utmost in old-fashioned luxury and elegance. Well-polished brass railings, mid-Victorian style in architecture, furniture, etc. Bedrooms twelve feet high and twenty-five feet square, overlooking St. Stephen's Green. (I wake up to the sound of birds crying in the green and look down on a mother-duck followed by her young, tranquilly gliding along a little stream.) Dining-room redecorated in Adam style. All around us streets like those of lower New York as it used to be. Great repose in atmosphere, motor-horns muted, busses quiet.

Needing a haircut, I went into the "Gentleman's Haircutting Saloon" opposite the Shelbourne. The barber, a small archaic Irishman, asked me where I had had my hair cut last. "In New York," said I. Said he, "I thought so," implying that there was a great deal amiss with New York.

So it appears when the name of Mayor O'Dwyer comes up in conversation. He is notorious in Ireland, having been born in Drogheda, I think. The Irish are all ashamed of him and ashamed in general of the goings-on of Irish-American politicians. I am told that the Irish government, being so new, is still innocent of all corruption.

The Irish regard the Irish-Americans as of a totally different race, and I think of the "Shamrock Hotel" that one Glenn McCarthy has just built in Houston, Texas. This "multi-millionaire wild-catter" oil-man goes in, I read the other day, for "big-name dinner-entertainers," and a filet mignon costs eleven dollars in his twenty-one million dollar palace hotel. How unlike the genie in the bottle is the genie out of the bottle whom we see on our side of the Atlantic.

Meanwhile, there is no doubt a chip on the general shoulder of Ireland, and the war of independence against England still goes on. I noted on the "Britannic" a scorn of Ireland and the Irish. The purser had no Irish money to give me and no time-table of trains from Cobh to Dublin, although the Cunarders have been stopping for generations at Queenstown. Just so, there seems to be a studied indifference to England in Ireland, while every secret of American life is well-known here.

At the Shelbourne, I see at a neighbouring table a grizzled bespectacled man, with a straggling grey beard and the air of a scholar. I take him at once for a professor at some French provincial university. Now he turns out to be an American, and not only that but a lawyer from Newburgh-on-the-Hudson bearing my name. We are fourth or fifth cousins. He gives me a book of poems he has written and says he has come to Ireland for two reasons, to see a skylark rise in the air singing and to hear "the best English spoken anywhere." He heard this on Sunday in the sermon at the Church of Ireland cathedral of St. Patrick. Is there, in fact, anything more charming than the well-tempered Irish voice?

The Shelbourne begins to fill up with characters from Somerville and Ross, "Ascendancy" families and dispossessed county families who represent the great Irish hunting and horse-breeding interest. But, on the whole, I am less interested in the hunters than in the hunted, man and beast.

I have presented some of the letters that my friend of forty years, Padraic Colum, gave me in New York, the Padraic Colum whom Frank O'Connor described once as "another Goldsmith,—he has the same midland background of gentle fields and the same gift of absolute pitch, of being always able to give out the middle C of literature." One of these letters was to Thomas MacGreevy, director of the National Gallery of Ireland, who was having all the pictures rehung on newly gilded walls. He asked me about the re-hanging of the Metropolitan Museum in New York, and, when I said the walls there were grey, he answered, "Yes, and, begging your pardon, too Protestant for me." He showed me a fine portrait of Oliver Cromwell which he had hung "in the best light," i.e., in almost total darkness, down by the baseboard and behind a door. Easy to understand how the Irish feel about this Puritan who offered in Ireland a bounty of five pounds "for the head of a wolf or a priest." MacGreevy said I had not realized the effect on Henry James of James's Irish papist forbears. (They were actually of the straitest sect of Presbyterians, although one of our exegetical critics has spoken of James as a "crypto-Catholic.") It was the papist forbears who inspired, he said, the chapter on Chartres in *A Little Tour in France* and his account of riding in a sedan chair. MacGreevy showed me two pictures signed "P.V.," convinced that they were Paolo Uccellos, and, among many fine Spanish works, three Goyas. He said he had seen me in London in 1926 in Leonard Woolf's office;—he was going out and saw my card as I went in.

The Puritanism of the Irish, so like and so unlike our own, comes down, according to Sean O'Faolain, from the early cenobites. Among them the ideal of self-mortification and penance ran wild, and they provided inmates for all the monasteries and hermits for the islands off the Irish and Scottish coasts. One of them hung for seven years from hooks under his armpits, another lay the first night in the same grave with every corpse brought to his church. Still another sat for seven years on the backbone of a whale.

In his pretty garden at Dun Leoghaire, Sean O'Faolain says there are two governments in Ireland, the Dail and the Church. Each of these checkmates the other. We can see this now when the Bishop of Galway is killing Dr. Brown's Maternity Bill, which subsidizes maternity and attempts to put an end to the scandalous infant-mortality rate. This bill would interfere with the control of the family by the Church.

Miss Ria Mooney of the Abbey Theatre takes us to the fashion show at the Hotel Gresham, the first show of the kind ever held in Ireland. A troop of pretty girls, smart and well-groomed, products of a new school for mannequins, displayed costumes of the lovely Irish tweeds in a hundred shades and as fine as silk. President O'Kelly was there, applauded when he rose. This is one of the notes of the new

Republic of Ireland, like the industrial exhibition we saw
the other day, showing all the new Irish manufactures, plumb-
ing, farm-machinery and I don't know what. Strange, for I
have not seen in the country, south of Belfast, the smoke of
a single factory-chimney.

To the Pearl Lounge, a rendezvous of the Dublin intellectuals, where I met many of the new writers. It was cold
and damp on this May evening, and we all sat about with
overcoats on. There was Robert Smylie, the editor of the
Irish Times, a big bulky man and a Presbyterian. This is all
the more paradoxical when the editor of the London *Times*
is, in his turn, a Roman Catholic.

I remember what L. A. G. Strong wrote in *The Sacred
River*, "Ireland in the twentieth century is no place for an
Irish writer to live in. Ireland today persecutes every writer
who is not content to make his act of submission and accept
a censorship which in this country, England, would be
thought excessive for a girls' school." That brings back what
my old friend F.H. told me. He had gone to live in Wexford
where he tried to start with his friends a conversation club
to meet once a week. But for this he was obliged to get the
bishop's permission, and the permission was refused.

No wonder Arland Ussher can be called "the only philosopher in Ireland." Yet writers, in this highly articulate country, continue to abound. Everyone, moreover, seems to be self-
possessed. There is no self-consciousness, such as we have at
home, on the part of any type, class or person. Barring an
occasional shyness, everyone is forthright. Complete aplomb
prevails on every hand.

But my new friend Monk Gibbon says, "The heroic imagination has gone, which means that at least half our mental

life is dead"; and AE once wrote to me, "We in Ireland are reacting against the idealism which led us to war and civil war and I fear we are in for an era of materialism. In Ireland we have a natural apathy about literature. It began to descend on us after we became self-governing. Before that we were imaginative dreamers." In a similar strain, Molly Colum wrote to me from Ireland two years ago, "This country is strange and lovely, but the old life is all gone. The government is shockingly efficient and is possessed of a fury for cleaning, fixing and building. They have cleared away the old bookstalls from the Liffey quays that used to make that part of the town like a bit of Paris. There is hardly a slum left. The government hasn't quite got out to the West yet, but they have made a beginning by cleaning up the very old fishing village of the Claddagh outside of Galway where people used to have their own customs, dress and wedding ceremonies. The whole intellectual life is dimmed beyond recognition."

We lunch at the University College, founded by Cardinal Newman, with Francis MacManus and the President, Dr. Tierney, a great Greek scholar. Dr. Tierney took us round the buildings through lofty graceful rooms with marble mantelpieces and ceilings decorated in low relief. There were recessed niches everywhere to hold statuettes. A small round table set for five in the beautiful Apollo room, with figures on the walls of muses and graces made by Italian plasterers for one of the bucks of the Regency time.

As we were parting on the porch, a beggar-woman came up and besought us for money: "Poor old granny I am. I'm cold." But this type of the "crazy old Irishwoman," familiar to my childhood in the United States, has almost disappeared from the streets of Dublin. One seldom sees the workhouse paupers who appear in Liam O'Flaherty's *The Tramp*. How Gorky-esque, how Russian, this writer makes them, like many of the people in O'Flaherty's *The Informer*. It seemed to me that Gallagher, the revolutionary leader in this play, was modelled on Turgenev's Bazarov. How well I remember the drizzling rain in front of the pub and the huge brutal clown, the informer, with his little round hat perched on his massive skull.

But many of the old Irish types we used to meet or hear about seem now to have disappeared. There were the Irish vagabond scholars with whom as a young man I worked in New York. They all knew Greek as well as Latin, they were usually besotted, with broken shoes, and one of them had served in the French Foreign Legion. Then there were the hangers-on one met in fashionable circles, pets of the rich, great spongers who paid their way as gossips, wits and drawing-room entertainers; and there were the shabby-genteel poor relations like Colonel Stephens whom I used to see in London. He made a small income as a spy working for the French government watching the Germans in restaurants there, kicked down stairs now and then by some swell whom he had libelled. It is obvious that the new Irish republic has put an end to these types or at least increased their self-respect.

But how much has Ireland really changed? I was reading the other day Henry Osborn Taylor's *The Mediæval Mind*. Taylor says that the old Irish heroic tales are full of truculence, irra-tionality, hyperbole and *non-arrival*. In certain tales the *un-steadfast* purpose is notable, "the hero quite forgetting the initial motive of his action." There are on every page "the makings of a brawl."

With all their "cleverness, facility, ardour and energy," in disseminating early Christianity, the deficiency of the old Irish was lack of organization, and they had but little capacity for ordered discipline humbly and obediently accepted for others. Therefore they ceased to lead or even keep pace with others after the first period of evangelization in Western Europe, when what was required was "united and persistent effort for order." Thus Henry Osborn Taylor. Does this partially explain what Toynbee calls the "abortive western Celtic civilization"? Irish art, architecture, writing, philosophy all "ran down like a clock and stopped" after the great efflorescence of the sixth and later centuries.

Of course, the Irish are still turbulent and bellicose, but they take it out in a black eye and seldom go in for murder. I remember reading in a newspaper once that, after 1920, they closed twenty-one gaols in Ireland because they had no one to put in them. But in a play I have just seen, an old woman character, with her arms on her hips, trails her shawl with bravado. In all her gestures were "the makings of a brawl."

What wonderful memories I have of the Irish players, the best, or almost, I ever saw, though I don't forget Copeau's Vieux Colombier or the Russian players whom I also saw in New York. Copeau spent $40 on his décor where the Americans spent $40,000, because they couldn't believe in the play or the actors and had to conceal their doubts with a splendour of equipment. As for the Russians, there was never anyone like Olga Knipper, Chekhov's widow, dowdy enough off the stage but on the stage, in a Turgenev comedy, a radiant young countess. She was possessed by her characters and really protean. How different from our "star" system in which the actress must always be her much-advertised self, whether on or off the stage, and attract all the attention even when others at the rear are doing the business.

Now in Ireland, it may be that the great writers are dead; but with what gusto, at the Gate Theatre, they have just played *The School for Scandal,* and how beautifully natural they are at the Abbey. J. B. Yeats used to say that the Irish were natural writers of plays, for they are all lovers of dialogue who enjoy their neighbours as they watch, as it were, the drama of life. Now Bryan MacMahon tells me of his group of players in Listowel, and a young man from Kilkenny says that every Irish town has a similar group made up of the local tradespeople.

Monk Gibbon takes me to lunch at Trinity College with the Greek scholar, Professor Stanford. On the wall of the dining-room was a portrait of Sir J. P. Mahaffy, the Greek scholar of earlier days, the provost of the college, to whom, when I was fifteen, I had the effrontery to write, asking for his autograph. After lunch Professor Stanford shows us in the Library the Book of Kells, taking it out of the case and turning the pages.

Mahaffy and Edward Dowden were the bigwigs of Anglo-Irish culture, and of Dowden I heard much from J. B. Yeats when I too was living at Petitpas' in New York. Dowden was one of the early admirers and correspondents of Whitman,—so was J. B. Yeats, who later turned against the "emotional man" and caricatured him in drawings in letters to me; but Dowden, the pioneer in the cult of Whitman, was totally indifferent to the Irish literary revival and to the recovery of the ancient Irish heritage during the years of preparation for it. He dissuaded Aubrey de Vere from wasting his time on any Irish heroic subject, and, in order to become another student of Wordsworth and Shakespeare, turned away contemptuously from everything Ireland had produced. He belittled the "mere" Irish element and failed to encourage in any way the Irish literary pioneers; and he paid the penalty, as John Eglinton says, in the isolation of his later years and in the oblivion that descended after his death upon his personality and name.

How like our Anglo-American critics of the time when I was growing up and when our modern literature was brewing,— I mean Brownell, Woodberry and Barrett Wendell who described Stephen Crane's work as "sensational trash." We too had a still colonial academic tradition, one that had little or no relation to the springs of our own life and the new American writers who were going their own way. We had, in short, like Ireland, what Thomas MacDonagh called "a full-grown criticism side by side with a baby literature," and Brownell, Wendell and Woodberry saw the movement of their time only as it were across a gulf. These critics were too inelastic to adapt themselves to a polyracial American literary future, and they clung, as conscious colonials, to their mother England. Yet in other respects they were as American as Dowden was Irish at the time when W. B. Yeats, the son of his great friend J. B. Yeats, crossed over the Pale and made Anglo-Irish literature more Irish than the Irish themselves. As my old friend Ernest Boyd said, "Irish" Ireland was known to Dowden "only as a strange country where poverty, moonlighting, rebellion and ignorance survived"; and he was, like our American critics, "a provincial, treading at a respectful distance in the wake of his superiors."

The old guide at the Guinness Brewery, formerly a worker there, contentedly speaks of porter as "the workingman's drink." Then, without any colour of animus, he refers to stout as "the drink of the upper classes."

All this as if the question of classes had been settled when men were living in caves, as if upper and lower were as plain as black and white. Nor was there any suggestion here of the sometimes hypocritical effort, across the Atlantic, to wipe out these distinctions. Social rebellion seems to be unknown in this nation of historic rebels,—but rebels only against the English.

We have called upon Jack B. Yeats at the Portobello Nursing Home (formerly the Portobello Hotel). Sunset light out of his top-story corner window over the Grand Canal. The swans had just been placed in the canal today. Jack Yeats, who had displaced a tendon in his back, seemed to be a great pet in the nursing home. He received us in a large square well-appointed hospital room with a wood fire in the grate. He is shorter than his father, with a big bony nose and jutting chin such as his father may well have had, concealed by the long white beard. He was dressed with a careless old-fashioned elegance in a black-and-white checked shawl-coat, with a pearl scarf-pin in his black tie and well-polished pumps. He offered us sherry and Irish whiskey.

Jack Yeats is seventy-six years old. His wife died four years ago, his last sister Lily a year ago, and he has no children. He talked much about his father, the "governor," who had a Dublin studio in York Street, with a beautiful eighteenth-century mantelpiece. At breakfast he would read passages of poetry, never because of its speculative interest, for he disliked all abstractions. He read out the first speeches of the *Prometheus Unbound* but never the ecstatic lyricisms of the famous fourth act. He thought Keats a greater poet than Shelley because he was more concrete. Once J. B. Yeats had brought home, when they lived in London, in Bedford Park, the poet of the Sierras, Joaquin Miller, whom Jack Yeats remembered as a cross between Walt Whitman and Buffalo Bill. He thought Joaquin was his mother's idea of a real poet. Jack Yeats greatly admired Bret Harte and painted one of his best pictures as a tribute to him. It is now owned in Belfast by a rich Jewish patron who has a whole roomful of Jack Yeats's pictures. He spoke of his sister as a great "remembrancer"; she had done his remembering for him, whereas he was very vague about family affairs. But he remembered hearing how, during the great famine, his grandfather, a clergyman in County Down, in a very poor Roman Catholic district, had conducted a christening in secret, feeling that he could not make a public celebration of it. He said his father's best pictures were in Charlemont House, where I had already seen them, though the family pictures were in the National Gallery of Ireland. This gentle old man with his courtly manner and charming smile seemed sad and much older than his years in appearance.

Jack Yeats is now by far the most famous painter in Ireland. One sees his pictures everywhere. His later phase is decidedly of the French impressionist type, suggesting Monet, the drawing somewhat obscured in a confusion of colours. In his early work one saw national types, men in carts, playing cards in boats, going to the fair or the races, out-door Irish life, barefooted children, mountain landscapes, horses with heads high, proud, and with flowing manes. Like his old broadsides, these pictures were boldly outlined, reflecting his lifelong passion for Daumier and Goya. One felt in them the affinity between Ireland and Spain and also what Padraic Colum calls "the secret that the Irish are a youthful people and that they are outside the great tiresome states that make the Byzantium of the West."

Our kind friend Monk Gibbon takes us to call upon Mrs. Yeats in Rathmines. We are driven there by the young poet John Ryan, the editor of the little magazine "Envoy." Mrs. Yeats is English, broadly built, with white hair, cordial and direct in manner. She remembers me as a friend of her husband's father, and she shows me, hanging near the front door, J. B. Yeats's last portrait of himself, the one I used to see, never finished, in his room at Petitpas'. The house, in which the poet Yeats never lived, contains all of her husband's books in two large rooms, overlooking a well-cared-for garden. Engravings of Blake cover the walls, seven illustrations of Dante and all the engravings for the Book of Job. Mrs. Yeats has Yeats's notebooks and Lily Yeats's diary. In the basement two sad-looking women were making Christmas cards on the old printing press of the Cuala Press that Miss Elizabeth Yeats once directed. Miss Yeats had bought the press for a few pounds in a little Irish town, where it had printed for many years the local weekly newspaper, and she had a good eighteenth-century font of type cast and the paper made from linen rags. Jack Yeats had drawn his broadsides for the press with designs for hand-coloured prints. Elizabeth Yeats herself had known nothing about the press-work. She disliked machinery and said she was afraid even of a sewing-machine. Her first helpers were children who had just left school.

Except as a listener at a lecture, I was never in the presence of the veiled and ambiguous personality of W. B. Yeats, but who could have doubted that he was an ever and ever greater and greater poet? When I wrote to John Eglinton, however, asking him how this wonderful writer happened to fall under the influence of the Americans Eliot and Pound, he replied, "Yeats was never a man of independent culture and so fell under the influence at all times of better-grounded minds like Lionel Johnson, Arthur Symons, etc."

How many family stories J. B. Yeats told me, the sort of stories that seldom get into biographies. As an artist in London, trying to make a living as an illustrator, he would come home in the evening to the house in Bedford Park. There his wife, lonely in her exile from Sligo, tended her flowers in window-boxes and fed the few poor birds that found their way in to a dim city window. One day, coming home, during those London years, he found Jack creeping about slowly on his hands and knees. "What are you doing?" he said; and Jack replied, "Trying not to get up an appetite." In the background was always their old servant Rose, who went with them every-where and who reminded me of my nurse Rosie, whose letters I used to address to her mother at "Sion Mills, County Tyrone."

J. B. would drag out of his pocket and read to me the letters, black from handling, he had received from his children. The only great portrait of J.B.'s I ever saw in America was his head of John O'Leary, haunting in its depth. One could never have guessed in New York, in Yeats's old age, how masterly were the portraits I have now seen in the Dublin galleries, really a history of Irish culture in his time. Shallow beside them were the portraits of Lavery and Orpen.

Mr. "Con" Curran,—C. P. Curran of Rathgar,—drives us over the Wicklow Hills where men in the bogs were cutting peat. He takes us to Glendalough, and there across the lake we saw St. Kevin's cave on the opposite slope. Now Curran writes to me about J. B. Yeats, who left Ireland at seventy and came to New York, where he died at eighty-three: "My wife was al-most the last to see him. She met him in St. Stephen's Green and he challenged her to admire his new suit of clothes. She knew that some nice old ladies, concerned that such an artist had not been to Italy, had put up a little money to permit him to see at least Florence and the Pre-Raphaelites. The old man stretched out his arms with his new plumage and said he was going to

New York in the morning. 'I may make my fortune there,' he said." His gaiety and what he called his "angel of impecuniosity" captivated me in New York. For years I thought impecuniosity was angelic, that poverty was the only fit condition for an artist or a writer.

I am invited to call upon "Seamus O'Sullivan,"—Dr. James Sullivan Starkey, the editor of the *Dublin Magazine*,—an elegant old gentleman still "attuned," as Padraic Colum says, "to Montaigne's astringent mode." He is seventy-one years old, a great collector of Oliver Goldsmith and the husband of the painter Estella Solomons. He showed me her portraits, very good, of Jack Yeats, Padraic Colum, James Stephens, etc. He also showed me his pictures by AE and one or two pictures painted by W. B. Yeats. AE dedicated his last three books to Dr. Starkey, and he has the copies of my books inscribed to AE. He was surprised that I never met AE who had spoken of me, he said, often.

I have scarcely ever had any letters that moved me as much as AE's. In one, written from the lake in Donegal where he had a cottage, he said, "I got my poems there. My friends fished for trout. I fished by the margin of the great deep which is the only fishing I can wait patiently at for months." In another he wrote, "I feel that Henry James had a mission pursued in spite of himself, the mission of Mark Twain, Walt Whitman, Vachel Lindsay, Carl Sandburg and other American writers which I think is to cut the umbilical cord connecting spiritually the new world with the old. Twain did it with irreverence, James through disillusionment, Whitman by new forms and by being a positive creator." I can't help resenting Arland Ussher's description of AE as,—no doubt a sage,—but a "bombinating" talker. He was very close to Thoreau and Emerson, not least in his agreement with the Oriental doctrines that formed the basis of the Hermetic Society (the root of the Irish literary revival). Yeats said this society had done more for Irish literature than Trinity College in three centuries. A great believer in democracy in the economic life, AE was also for the aristocratic intellect, ideals, poetry and the imagination as the qualities to be looked for in leaders. In all this he reversed the practical American point of view, while he reflected the half-mystical views of Thoreau and Emerson.

I believe the best modern readers of our greatest writers have been Irish. Everyone knows how J. B. Yeats read *Walden* to his son, the poet, who, in consequence of this, wrote *Innisfree*. Then AE and John Eglinton were closely connected in feeling and thought with Emerson, Thoreau and Whitman. John Eglinton,—W. K. Magee,—an old Unionist, has been living in England since the treaty of 1921. It was this Irishman who said, "Mankind may weary of the whole scheme of things at present," and who suggested that we might well expect a new crusade of some new Peter the Hermit.

The mystical note is still strong in Ireland,—a note of many types,—among the Protestants as among the Catholics, who keep up their pilgrimages to Loch Derg (mentioned by Dante). After a vigil in the Basilica they spend three days there on the rocks of the island lashed with rain, stumbling on bleeding knees up steep and slippery places, meditating on the Passion.

Again the kind Monk Gibbon takes us to Roebuck House to call, in Dundrum, upon Maude Gonne, Madam MacBride. She lives there with her son, the present minister of Foreign Affairs. The gate lets us into a big unkempt meadow with the vast old stables at the rear,—the weathervane is a figure of Mercury. The house stands to the right, a large early nineteenth century brick dwelling of Ascendancy grandeur. The paint has been scratched off the front door by the dogs. A grandson lets us into the dark entry,—it is twilight outside,— apologizing for leaving us alone with his grandmother: the maid and all the family have had to be out. He takes us into a large room at the rear, and then he goes off for an evening of electioneering.

The grand old lady is stretched out on a chaise longue, facing the coal fire. She is smoking a cigarette and reading a French yellowback novel. She seems to be glad to see us. "How kind you are," she exclaims, "to come and see a deaf old woman!" She has bold features and deep-set eyes, with a high-bred manner and charming gestures, her voice very distinguished and she herself full of humour. She had been trained to be an actress and one could see how beautiful she had been. She spoke at once of Yeats,—"Willie,"—whom she had known at twenty, he being at that time twenty-one: they had been constantly together but, as she said, "like brother and sister,"— there had evidently been no shred of romantic feeling on her side. Willie was then a student in a school of art and John O'Leary's most hopeful recruit.

Then she spoke of the peasant evictions as having set her off on the career that had been for her inevitable. Her mother had died when she was four, and she was brought up by a nurse at Howth. She played with the poor little neighbour children and learned to love them; and when the evictions came in the eighteen-eighties she saw these same people with their houses burned over their heads, left to starve by the tens of thousands. She saw a woman with a day-old baby left by the roadside and little children trying to kindle a fire in the rain. The landlords were destroying the homesteads because they could make more money by cattle-raising, and she knew then that Ireland must "leave the empire." Besides, she had been brought up in France and had become a republican there. No doubt she dramatized herself as a kind of Irish Joan of Arc who had set out to save her country. She told us how she stopped the famine in County Mayo, demanding for each person a shilling a day as well as seed-potatoes to plant in their cottage gardens. She had assembled ten thousand peasants and confronted the Governor with them and her demands. He had only ten policemen to hold them in check, and she was able to say there would be bloodshed unless the government agreed to her terms. She said she had really done very little but had no choice not to do it, and she had "never been afraid of anything." When her mother died, her father had taken her into the room before the coffin was closed, and she had heard him say, more to himself than to her, "Never be afraid of anything, even of death." After that, whenever she began to feel fear, she had thrown back her head. Her father had tried to stop her work in Ireland and cut off her allowance when she protested against the evictions; but later her father had joined her, moved as she had been, resigned from the British army and entered Irish politics. Three weeks after that he died.

Her memory was still perfect. If she had not had trouble with her heart, she would still be, at eighty-seven, as active as ever. She was evidently proud of her son who is doing just what she would like to be doing herself. She feels that the success of the republic is "wonderful" and says that in Ireland now no one needs to "starve."

A day at Bective, in County Meath, with Mary Lavin and her husband in their new white house, the "Abbey Farm." The ruins of the old abbey are in a ploughed field a few yards away. What an exceedingly pretty young woman and what a beautiful writer, actually born near Boston and an emigrant in reverse. She regrets the passing of the Ascendancy, with its fine manners, and the absence in England of her neighbour Lord Dunsany, the inventor of a theogony, a whole mythology, like Melville in *Mardi* and James Branch Cabell.

The long avenue of Bective House was lined with myriads of daffodils. It was like the beginning of a Turgenev story, "In the springtime, in a beechen grove"; and there, in the driveway before the house, raking the gravel, was old Kevin, the gardener, who remembered our friend James Stern,—born in this house,—when he was a boy. "Ah, Master Jimmie," said the old man; "he was a wild little boy. They had to send him away to live on a farm." That was at least thirty-five years ago, and Kevin had been raking the gravel long before that. Below the terrace lay the river Boyne, filled with rushes, and beyond rose the hill of Tara where the harp hung in the *Irish Melodies*. Only earthworks remain there; nothing is left of the "walls."

The harp is still a magic symbol. My wife has an old Egan harp, made about 1800, rather warped and with most of the strings gone. However, it occurred to us to take it to New York and ask at the Metropolitan Museum where it could be restrung. We drove up Madison Avenue through ever-thickening crowds and then set out to walk over to Fifth Avenue. I carried the harp over my shoulder. But we could not cross the streets,— a parade was coming. What a coincidence! We had not known it was St. Patrick's day. Then an Irish policeman caught sight of the harp and beckoned us forward; the crowd opened before us like the Red Sea before the Israelites, and people on all sides exclaimed at the sight of the old Irish harper,—namely, myself. A little boy asked me where the harp came from, and when I said Dublin he murmured in awe, "Dublin city! My father was born in Dublin city!"

We have been visiting in County Down, where my step-sister lives and where "the mountains of Mourne sweep down to the sea." Another world entirely, an Anglo-Irish military world. We are taken to a castle near by with sixty-three bedrooms and a library as large as the rotunda of the Library of Congress, filled with thousands of splendid morocco-bound books. But what a dwelling to fall heir to in the nineteen-fifties! Our hostess has cut in two the vast dining-room with a line of china-closets. On one side hang the family portraits of Kneller, Lely and Sir Thomas Lawrence, on the other she has installed her cooking-range and washing-machine. The family live in screened-off compartments in one of the former drawing-rooms, each one as large as an ordinary house.

A few days in the west of Ireland, and we drive up into Connemara, all one big green farm, as Ireland seems to be everywhere, with donkeys, pigs and chickens astray on the roads and tinkers and gypsies in caravans camping by the road-sides. One could imagine there all the tramps of Synge's plays, the itinerant pedlars and blind beggars on the highway and the black Spanish types that often remind one of Goya and the early broadsides of Jack B. Yeats.

In Galway, Lord and Lady Killanin took us for an all-day drive, with a picnic lunch, in County Clare. We spread out the baskets near the graveyard in the ruins of the Seven Churches. At one moment we stopped in the grounds of Lady Gregory's house, which has been torn down since her death, and we found the great beech-tree with the initials carved in the bark of all the writers,—G. B. S., W. B. Y., G. M., and I don't know how many others,—who had stayed there in Lady Gregory's time. Then on a small country road we drew up suddenly two yards away from Yeats's tower, with the dedication to his wife on a tablet in the wall. The tower was going back to the ruin the tablet prophesied for it, with the door half open and swinging in the wind. We climbed up through the three stories and looked down from the top. The walls were painted within a rather lurid blue that had some astrological or mystical significance.

How strange were the vast expanses of rock through which we drove in County Clare, with tombs of the Bronze Age scattered all about. They were dolmens of the sort one sees at Stonehenge and in some cases had never been disturbed. We saw castles in all stages of development, beginning with the pre-castle stage, a simple enclosure with a wall of stones. There were no modern buildings anywhere in sight to mark the changing centuries or suggest the passing of time. It was as if nothing had happened in twelve hundred years or four thousand years, as if pre-history and the Dark Ages still continued there and the people of those times had simply withdrawn for a day.

CHAPTER XII

IN FRANCE AND ITALY

Jo Davidson wrote to Dublin to welcome us to Europe,—"for I presume," he said, "that Dublin still considers itself part of Europe or at least the world." So, after a month in England, we went to France to stay with Jo and Florence, fourteen miles from Tours, in their Manoir de Becheron at Saché. It was three miles from the loveliest of the châteaux, Azay-le-Rideau. Jo had returned to France after seven years in America, caught and exiled there by the second world war, and he found that the French government had packed away all his sculpture in sixty-five cases in order to safeguard it from the German invaders. It was as if he had died and come home again and fallen heir to his own past, the whole work of his lifetime, where nothing had changed and where the old gardener, the old cook and Gino, his assistant, had watched over the pictures, the books and the grounds. We had the rooms in which Jo's friend Lincoln Steffens had written his autobiography a few years before.

It was in America, at the beginning of the forties, that Jo had knocked on my door at Weston. He was eager to love and to be loved, and we resumed in a moment the intimacy of the far-off time when I had been teaching in 1914 near London.

Spending his affection on Russia too, he was taken for a Communist, for he was possessed by that nostalgia for "the home that had never been a home" which Emma Goldman attributed to all Russian Jews. Even his friend Henry Wallace was also called a Communist, the man who had never read a line of Marx's writings and who made long speeches out of quotations from the Bible,—Henry Wallace of whom AE had written to me, "I found behind all his economics and agricultural science a lovely flower of mysticism." With his prodigious energy, Jo had gone into politics, getting up a gigantic organization to reëlect Franklin Roosevelt. I had gone with him to the White House where the President received us, with others including Joe Cotton and Dorothy Gish. There was also in this delegation a Polish opera-singer who said to Dorothy Gish on the station platform, "Why have you never married? You know everybody has a chance!" which struck me as a rather egregious remark to make to a charming woman of the stage. I had never heard of Joe Cotton, but we had no sooner got out of the taxi, on an apparently empty street, than a swarm of "bobby-soxers" gathered about him. Clamouring for his autograph, they had materialized from nowhere.

Meanwhile, Jo Davidson had made a bust of Helen Keller, with her hands eagerly raised, and he introduced me to this legendary character who had recently come to live in Westport. Helen and Polly, as we always called them,— for Polly Thomson, the Scottish companion, was Helen Keller's indispensable *alter ego*,—had also stayed at Becheron a year before we went there and Jo had painted a portrait of them talking. When they were not occupied with this conversation piece, they wandered together in the garden or strolled in the fields, blue with corn flowers and red with poppies, and in the evening they read together, Polly reading Wells's autobiography and Helen, in braille, *Candide* and Anatole France. They dabbled a little in Rabelais, who was born near by, at Chinon, near the ruined castle that Jo took us to see, and Jo had been at his best with Helen, delighting in the spring of joyousness that bubbled, at the slightest pressure, up to the surface. For Helen radiated happiness, as we had seen in Westport. There, with Jo and Gaetano Salvemini, the old anti-fascist professor at Harvard, we had all met again and again. Salvemini was publishing his "News from Italy" in which we still seemed to hear Mazzini anathematizing another Italian despot; and, of Helen, Polly said, "In all these forty years there hasn't been a day when I have not been amazed by something she has said or done." Now Salvemini, who had returned to Florence, arranged to have Helen "see" the Michelangelo tombs in the Medici chapel. Jo drove down with her, stopping on the way at Genoa to rescue Helen from a *soi-disant* cousin. This lady, eager to claim relationship with such a famous person, had invited Helen to come for a visit. She had married an Italian count, but her original name was Keller, and, like Helen's remote forbears, she had come from Switzerland, the rest being all guess-work and pretension. The lady was not even present when Helen, ready for any adventure, arrived at the palace where Jo found her, and she turned out to be an active fascist who had been a friend of Mussolini. After Helen and Polly left, she sent them a bill for the note-paper they had used there! As for the Medici tombs, Jo said he had never seen them so intimately as when he watched Helen's hands wandering over the forms. A moving scaffold was set up for her to stand on. She had, Salvemini said, ten eyes for sculpture, an art she had always loved and even practised.

Jo had come to visit us in a house we rented in northern Connecticut but, having lived so long in France, he did not

like villages built of wood, even the pretty Palladian village of
Cornwall. Nor had I, once upon a time, before I lived through
in imagination the life that lay behind this wooden village.
Only then did I understand why Walter Gropius came to feel
that wood was the right material for American building. Jo had
made, first or last, wonderful speaking likenesses of many of the
great persons of his time, from Winston Churchill and Anatole
France to Gandhi and Madame Chiang Kai-shek, a "Chinese
cross between Madame Récamier and Claire Booth Luce." Jo
did not admire this lady who had spent a year in New York
and had never once visited Chinatown,—inhabited, she said,
only by coolies,—but she had made the Chinese people "re-
spectable" for the man in the street who had thought of them
as merely laundrymen and chinks. Jo, having sculptured busts
of the statesmen at Versailles, had flown to South America to
make busts of the Presidents, and he had gone to Jugoslavia for
a portrait head of Tito and found himself there surrounded
with sculptors. He said that some of his sitters were short
stories, while others were novels, and that it took two to make
a bust, the important thing being the rapport of the artist and
the sitter; and Jo remarked that the reason why he was not
going to be a writer was that when he wrote he could not sing.
Arnold Bennett had told him he talked so well he could never
write, and yet he was at work on his autobiography,—*Between
Sittings* it was called. He had been getting to feel that he was
Atlas carrying the world,—"like that old gink in the picture
with his feet in the clouds,"—so he bent down, stepped out
from under, stood back and watched, and the world did not
budge a fraction of an inch.

After we left Saché, Jo flew to Israel to spend seven weeks
making busts there, enthusiastic over a country so full of youth
and courage, with so many new types for him to sculpture.

The extremes met there, Jews from the darkest holes of Asia and the most cultivated Jews from America and Europe. He worked in Beersheba on one of the frontiers and spent a week at a coöperative farm near the Sea of Galilee, and he visited several outpost settlements in the vast and rather terrifying desert and dashed up to Jerusalem to make a bust of Weizmann. There were also towns where they were building three houses a day blown up with cement out of a gun. He drove about the country, sometimes in a police jeep, sometimes in a luxurious car with a tub of clay in the baggage compartment, and whenever he saw a new type, a shepherd on the plain, a Yemenite, a Persian or an Indian Jew, Jo jumped out of the car and asked him to pose. He said that in Israel they couldn't believe he was a Jew, for never for a moment in his life had he felt an inferiority-complex. He did busts of the President, the cabinet, and even one of the Arab sheiks. "You can't stop him," Florence wrote about this mad escapade. In fact, he worked furiously, like a man out of his head, and he himself wrote, "We are exhausted, but it was worth it,"—or would have been if it had not killed him. He had received his book at Tel Aviv and found it was full of changes,—paragraphs had been added,—it was no longer his book; and, terribly agitated, he slashed away at it while his bronchitis turned into pneumonia. He had come home to Saché and had been taken to the hospital at Tours. There, quite suddenly, he died.

Jo was one of the great talkers, sometimes tumultuous, usually keen, all gusto, mimicry and humour, now and then recalling the great talkers of the past for whom conversation was one of the fine arts. But where he was spontaneous, they had been deliberate, preparing themselves for the breakfasts and dinners in which they were to take part and planning the conversation well in advance. They sometimes kept commonplace-books with notes of the remarks of distinguished men, volumes of whose table-talk were subsequently published, and it was largely because of the Boswells who abounded in those days that the lives of the great writers of the time were so clearly remembered. I have often wondered if our age would be known in the future at all, with so few talkers, diarists or letter-writers, with most communications uttered through the telephone or on postcards saying, "Wish you were here." Even in fiction there was less and less realism, recording any kind of significant life. I doubt if fine conversation is held in any esteem at all, for I remember Oliver Gogarty, the Irish poet, for whom there was apparently no place at New York dinner-tables. He was a classical table-talker of a sort that was well-known in the days of Dr. Holmes and Oscar Wilde, but who on Park Avenue cared for this? I gathered that Oliver Gogarty was lost in New York. Until he was picked up dying in the street, he went every night to a West Side saloon, a resort of Irish footmen, grooms and butlers with whom he talked till four or five in the morning. They knew good conversation if their employers did not.

Robert Flaherty took me to lunch once with Oliver Gogarty, who had a sharp word for everybody. He said that he and Joyce were walking in Dublin one day when they saw J. B. Yeats ahead of them,—Yeats whom Gogarty regarded as a bore, with his obsession of the "solitary man." Joyce said to Gogarty, "Let's touch him for a shilling." They did so and Yeats replied, "Certainly not, for, in the first place, I haven't got it, and in the second place, if I gave it to you, you and your friend would spend it for drink." Said Joyce in response to this, "It is not competent for us to discuss the future of a non-existing object." Then, always the scholastic, he added to Gogarty, "I gave him the Razor of Occam." I might have written down more of Gogarty's remarks had I not supposed that they would all appear in one of his books; but I remember his account of the burial of George Moore's ashes on an island in one of the Irish lakes. Gogarty rowed the boat over and George Moore's spinster sister, sitting in the stern, held the urn with the ashes in her lap. The day was warm and Gogarty, who had not rowed for forty years, took off first his tall hat, then his coat, then his waistcoat. At that point the spinster sister said, "I hope, Dr. Gogarty, you will not remove any further habiliments."

It was true that Gogarty talked only of Ireland and the literary revival there, and this might have been tiresome at dinner-tables. I asked him if he knew anything about a painter named H. Phelan Gibb, of whom I owned two or three pictures and who was one of the two painters of the time who "would be discovered after they were dead, they being predestined to a life of tragedy." So Gertrude Stein said in her autobiography, the other painter being Juan Gris, and she also said that Harry Gibb was her "first and best English friend" and that Gogarty was his great friend and patron. Gogarty professed not even to know his name, and he said, "There were so many of these fellows sitting on my doorstep." Neither then nor at any other time, though I wrote in all directions, could I find any trace of H. Phelan Gibb. In fact, what became of so many of the talents who abounded in Paris at that time? They disappeared utterly or ended now and then as attendants at Texas filling-stations.

A few years after visiting Jo Davidson at Saché, we spent a winter in Rome, where as a boy of thirteen, enthralled by Italian art, I had stayed in an English pension in the Piazza Poli. A priest from Australia who was there came back every night to report the proceedings of the canonization of Pio Nono, and he told us that the process failed when it was announced that the pope in question had taken snuff. After that winter I pored over Bernard Berenson's handbooks in their first burnt-sienna bindings, and during several years to come I read Ruskin, John Addington Symonds and Vernon Lee about whom I began to write. Then, when I went to Harvard, Berenson was already a legend partly because he had selected most of the pictures in Mrs. Jack Gardner's Fenway Court. There I had seen the lady whom he called Boston's pre-cinema star, seated on her throne, observing the observers. Fifty years later still I read Berenson again, at a time when he felt "out-moded in the Angry-Saxon world." He had retained his old belief in liberalism and humanism, and he corroborated my own feeling that these were permanent realities instead of what others regarded as Victorian illusions. I was all for his faith in "life-enhancement" as the final aim of art, the task of trying to humanize mankind, and there was something spacious, something Goethean, unique in our time, a marvellous breadth and freshness in his note. What vitality there also was in this man approaching ninety who was to be active still at ninety-three. Everyone who knew him told anecdotes about him, as, for example, when a guard found him asleep in the Yale Museum, where he had gone to see the Jarves collection. The guard woke him up and reprimanded him. "I am Mr. Berenson," the old man said, "and I'm privileged to sleep in any museum in the world." In the circle of my friends there were four of his regular correspondents, and he began to write to me after I had sent him a book with a few pages devoted to his own writing. He sent me four books of his, inscribing one with the Virgin Mary's words to Saint Bernard in a vision, *Bene scripsiti de me*.

Now, during this winter in Rome,—at the American Academy, where we knew Ralph Ellison and Theodore Roethke, that fine poet from the Far West,—Berenson wrote inviting us

to spend four days at his villa I Tatti in Settignano. We stopped
on the way at Lerici to see Percy Lubbock, who had also invited us for a three-day visit, but we suggested rather a lunch
on Sunday with this delightfully hospitable table-talker. With
his great prelatical belly, partially deaf, he lived in a pleasant
villa half-hidden in woods and hanging over the Mediterranean
sea, not far from the house where Shelley had spent several
months and much like the Californian coast at Carmel. But
when I spoke of this, Lubbock shuddered. Three young Eng-
lishmen, readers and amanuenses, sat at table with us; and we
regretted that we had to be on our way so soon, as we waved
good-bye in the rain to the solitary figure in the doorway.
Berenson's villa stood on a hill where Mark Twain had also
lived, like Leigh Hunt and John Addington Symonds before
him and where had supposedly also stood the villa in which
the tales of Boccaccio were told. We were given a beautiful set
of rooms hung with works of art,—among them a Nattier and
a Longhi,—like all the rooms and corridors, for the house was
a sort of museum especially of early Florentine and Siennese
masters. The frail and tiny little man, scarcely more than five
feet tall, moved swiftly, with bird-like steps and the silence of
a shadow, and at table he sat bolt upright and as if carved in
ivory, speaking with a clear and finished enunciation. Later,
with a plaid rug over his knees, concealing a hot-water bottle
in his lap, he received, like another Voltaire, the pilgrims from
all the world who filled the house at lunch, tea and dinner.
One was Arturo Loria, the Florentine professor, who translated
him into Italian and who died soon after; and there was Harold
Acton, who came to dinner one day, and whom we presently
went to see in his great villa on the via Bolognese. The kind
Harold Acton, with his Chinese mannerisms and his anachro-
nistic gargoyle smile, walking with fluttering hands and feet

turned out, had lived for a number of years in China. He was at work on a history of the Bourbons of Naples with whom I fear he sympathized.

Berenson's talk was all concrete,—he disliked what he called "metafussics,"—and, with his incessant activity of mind, he discussed all manner of subjects, science fiction, the history of trade, the Risorgimento. I did not understand his distrust of Mazzini and Garibaldi,—he seemed to feel that the Italian people had been better off before they were united,—and I could hardly believe that B.B. would have liked a time when Mazzini was imprisoned simply for being "a thinker." But there was great sweetness and liberality in almost all he said, and I could see why my friends George Biddle and Walter Pach always spoke of Berenson as "the dear old man." He quoted Ovid freely, with Platen and German poetry, and, deeply read in the history of the Fuggers and the Medici, he remarked that a knowledge of the history of trade was indispensable for one who wished to know art-history. I remembered what he had written somewhere, "I was born for conversation and not for writing books." In fact, he had written to me, "Comparing small with great, I should have had, like Saint Augustine, four or five amanuenses to take down talk. I am really a born talker, not a born writer."

He worked every morning on his three-volume catalogue of Italian paintings, hoping to complete it in three or four years. After that he expected to go back to writing. In addition, he kept a daily journal, one page each morning when he woke up, for he still lived wholly in the present and the future. Every day at 12:30 we met him at the front door and climbed into the old Ford station-wagon, driven by the stout Welsh chauffeur Parry, who had been in his employ for forty years. At a certain point we all dismounted for a walk, though, small as an atom and almost as light, he had expressed a fear that a wind might rise and blow him away. Standing on a ridge, he pointed to the city of Florence below, creeping out like a tide to swallow him up, and he was afraid it might engulf I Tatti if Harvard, to which he had left it, sold his land. One day the station-wagon stopped in a farm-yard,—one of those shabby half-deserted farm-yards that had once delighted Henry James,—and Berenson, drawing a great key out of his pocket, unlocked a green wooden gate in a high stone wall. He threw open the gate and there within stood the castle of Vincigliata, an old feudal stronghold, long a ruin, that had been restored by an eccentric Englishman a hundred years ago. This John Temple Leader had also built a romantic grey turret on the edge of a large dark rocky pool, the old quarry, no less, from which Donatello had got the *pietra serena* he used in his sculpture.

Berenson had been "in hiding" in the second world war, when he said he was a carbuncle on Mussolini's neck, and he showed in *Rumour and Reflection,* written at that time, how far outside of art he was accustomed to ranging. That book, he told me, had been refused by all the English and American publishers when another man came to see him, read it, accepted it and sold about twenty thousand copies: it had become the most popular of all his books. He was indignant with a young critic who had also come to see him and had betrayed his confidence about Santayana. The young critic had sworn not to mention Berenson's relations with Santayana, with whom he had never had a quarrel, but it was obvious that he disliked this other old savant of the time who had once been, like him, an "awe-stricken pilgrim" in Europe. Both of these men had crossed all the frontiers, but, while Salvemini was Berenson's dear friend,—that other great liberal and humanist,—he remembered William James's saying, "George keeps his heart on ice." Berenson remarked, "I would go further and say he had no heart,—he was all *pen* . . . There is a French saying, *Il gagne à être connu.* Of Santayana I would say, *Il gagne à ne pas être connu.*" I do not know whether there was anything personal in this adverse feeling, or in his memory of the il-liberal Irving Babbitt as a "dull heavy sulker," or in his remark that T. S. Eliot was his "mortal enemy." No one in Berenson's time at Harvard, alert and zestful as he might have been, felt that in youth there was anything to be envied. Youth was looked upon as a causeway between boyhood and manhood, not as a state that anyone wished to prolong, and no one whom Berenson remembered shared the cult of youth of Scott Fitz-gerald, Hemingway and Edna Millay. I recalled Joel Spingarn's essay on the fashionable theory of the twenties that all art and wisdom are the products of physical youth and that nothing can be really good unless men still young have done it or liked it.

Many scraps of Berenson's talk later came back to me, ob-servations that he made while I sat beside him or, now and then, in his letters. He said that as a boy in Boston he had gloated over *Cudjo's Cave* in a long forgotten monthly called *Our Young Folks.* He spoke of the well-known affinity between the English and the Arabs, from Sir Richard Burton to T. E. Lawrence, connecting this with the homosexuality that is sup-posed to flourish in English public schools. He was much taken with Mary MacCarthy, who had recently visited him,—"What a fascinating talker, and what a writer!" She had just published her book on Venice where he was presently going to revisit the glimpses of the moon and revise his own early handbooks. He was planning to spend the following summer rediscovering Florence, almost forgotten in years of travelling elsewhere. He said that, by way of "courting" him, Mabel

Dodge had remarked to him, "You are the greatest American since Abraham Lincoln." At the moment he was excited by a Chinese novel: "Never was I so admitted to the intimacy of the Chinese mind and heart." But Italy was never long out of his mind. When I sent him *The Dream of Arcadia,* he said that sixty years before he had urged his brother-in-law Logan Pearsall Smith to write about Americans in Italy. He continued, "On a lawn in front of the cemetery church at Ferrara there is (I hope still) a beautiful Canovaesque sarcophagus containing the body of a young Bostonian who died there in the twenties of the nineteenth century. As a Protestant he could not be buried in holy ground, in the cemetery itself. I have often itched to write a Pateresque imaginary portrait of this young pilgrim to the land of his spiritual ancestors." Berenson asked, "How early did continental Europe distinguish between an Englishman from Great Britain and one from America? Stendhal was perfectly aware of the difference." Again he wrote, "Why not make a study of the attitudes, I mean the conscious attitudes toward visual art in America during the last 150 years? How well prepared you are for doing it." The subject would have appealed to me in the days when I wrote the life of Symonds and hoped to write a study of Vernon Lee and when I opened *The Wine of the Puritans* with a note about Baja on an Italian midsummer afternoon. Berenson and his lovable companion, Nicky Mariano, wrote letters as kings and queens are supposed to do, as if *you* were the only person living.

Sometimes Berenson wrote to me from his woodsy retreat at Vallombrosa. There, surrounded by the forest, his only neighbours were the parish priest and the men who were in charge of the forest nursery garden. In his summer cottage, W. W. Story had died, and he said, "It was Story's book *Fiammetta* which ranked high among those that gave me a longing for

Italy." Already deaf, he feared that blindness was also coming on, and in that case he "would be as good as cut off from the Not-me . . . rather a dreary prospect for one who is still so passionately interested in the world at large as I am." Again he wrote from Tripoli, from the marvellous ruins of Leptis Magna, and I remembered what his wife said in *Across the Mediterranean* about an earlier journey to Tunisia and Algiers: "My husband was like a war-horse scenting the battle . . . His remorseless energy and curiosity invest every step of art-history with fascination . . . With his insatiable curiosity about the genesis, the affiliations, the inter-influence of all forms of art, [in museums] he is so full of excitement that he stays on and on, and is capable, even, of persuading the care-takers of out-of-the-way little collections to let him go on by the light of a candle when all the others are exhausted." Yet it was part of his great strength that, ranging over all the arts, he clung on the whole so closely to his own parish, Italian painting after and before Giotto. There was much in his career that was ambiguous, no doubt, but his interests were unques-tionably universal, and I could well believe what Edith Whar-ton is supposed to have said, "My other friends are ponds. Berenson is an ocean."

On that earlier visit to France, Gaetano Salvemini, Berenson's friend, had been a constant subject of talk at Saché. Jo David-son, who had loved Salvemini too, gave me a pencil sketch he had made of the great old man in Florence. He had put this in my hand when he came to see us off in Paris at the boat-train for Cherbourg, and the first person I saw on the ship, climb-ing the companionway, was Salvemini, no other. I held the drawing in front of him; he saw his own head with astonish-ment, and for the next five or six days, until we reached New York, we were all generally together. Tired of wandering,

Salvemini had lost the habit of staying in one place; he was on his way back to Harvard to arrange for the publication of his *Mazzini;* and the last I saw of him he was walking off the pier, with one small bag in his hand. This reincarnation of an antique sage, whom kings were eager to consult and who lived as far as one could without money or possessions, appropriately bore the name that in Apulia, where he had grown up, was the last word uttered when the fishing boats went out.

CHAPTER XIII

IN ENGLAND AND AFTER

Twice we visited England, once by way of Holland, where we spent a few days at the Hague and Amsterdam. Our ship followed the coast line from Le Havre, and, looking out of the porthole in the early morning, I saw a windmill and a cow and I knew we were approaching Rotterdam. At Haarlem, in the Groote Kerk, we heard a recital of the great church organ to which Mozart had listened,—it was played by the Dutch organist, Piet Kee,—and I remembered how my mother had taken me to hear it, and the great Swiss organ at Fribourg, when I was twelve. At Amsterdam we met Lewis Mumford's opposite number, Wijdeveld, the architect and city-planner, who had designed the interior of the "Nieuw Amsterdam," the ship on which we had crossed the ocean. Concerned with the town of the future, in which sunless houses and narrow airless streets would have ceased to exist, he was looking forward to a new renaissance transcending the scientific phase through which we were passing. He foresaw man's ultimate triumph over the machine and a day when ripeness and serenity of spirit would prevail, a new era, a new world order; and meanwhile he was building for a society of motor-cars, aeroplanes, films and sea-going liners. With Wijdeveld we went to see the exhibition of

Alexander Calder's immense "Black Spider" and other "sta-biles."

In England, where the vengeance bombs were falling in history and memory only,—a country I had not seen for twenty-five years,—I was again struck by the richness of a culture with which in the United States we had nothing to compare. In Salisbury, where we spent ten days, there were four bookshops, with the best second-hand bookshop I had ever seen, and, be-sides the Salzburg marionettes, there were three plays running at the time, a play of Aristophanes, a play about George Her-bert and *A Winter's Tale* in a private garden. Exquisitely acted this, and all by amateurs, with music by Purcell and Telemann, issuing from a hidden gramophone in a thicket by the river; moreover, with the loveliest English voices,—and all in a town of twenty thousand persons. At the same time, the spire of the cathedral was in danger of falling, as the walls of the abbey church at Bath seemed to be on the point of collapse, and I wondered how, with the burdens of the present, the English could preserve all these grand remnants of the Middle Ages. At Dorchester there were statues of Thomas Hardy and William Barnes; tablets were generally affixed to the houses of authors, and the Penguins reprinted, ten or twenty books at a time, a million copies of Shaw and Wells and Lawrence. One saw, at Hampton Court, the perpetual keeper of the vine, and the stately English language was still maintained in ordinary use, as in the sign one saw in St. Andrew's Square at Edinburgh, "The amenity of our streets is recommended to your care." I could have agreed with Lewis Mumford in his praise of Eng-land: "If I take England at her worst, in her rule over India, and if I add to it every crime, misery and brutality she has committed, I still see in the English, taken as a whole, the un-mistakable signs of a civilized people that is capable of self-cor-

rection and self-improvement, and that even in India has created
by her own example, her own ideas, the very power that is
equal to challenging her own regime." The British never fail
to respond to tales of solitary courage. They have made almost
a popular classic of *Sailing Alone Around the World,* so long
all but forgotten in its own country.

But it seemed to me that, in literature at least, England and
America were drifting further and further apart, when one
thought of the days of Shaw, Wells and Arnold Bennett who
seemed to include in their writings the United States also. With
little formal education,—and this was true of Kipling, George
Moore and W. B. Yeats,—these English authors, with their
broad human interests, seemed somehow close to America where
the mass of readers shared common assumptions and a common
intellectual language. Shaw and Wells had the American faith
in improvability, whereas the later writers had lost their feeling
for the widely human and were more and more public school
boys with the old school tie. They were not universal enough on
their own ground to meet the Americans on theirs. With socialism achieved in England, they did not have to defend it;
and, with the loss of the empire, they were driven to ride again
their aristocratic and reactionary hobbies. They discussed such
trivialities as "U" and "Non-U." They abounded in memories of
Eton, and their sympathies were of the upper class, occasionally
tempered, it is true, by communism; as the English government had turned to the left, the authors had turned to the
right, and, amusing as they might be, they spoke to the
American mind as the voices merely of a small European country. The American mind was still Cromwellian, the English
was cavalier again; and, with the new polyglot American types,
the ancestral bond had vanished in the younger generation.
To be sure, the superior culture of the English was still evident

enough. There were the novels of Aldous Huxley, so full of allusions and references to the history of painting and music, anthropology, zoology, of interest to all cultiviated people; and I remembered my first sight of the poet Auden in the Whitney Museum in New York. He had come to an exhibition of William Rimmer's drawings, and I recollect the absorbed curiosity with which he examined each and all. I wondered how many intellectual young Americans would have taken the trouble to examine the work of this little-known artist.

We lunched with Sir Desmond MacCarthy, who had been recently knighted and who did not encourage the use of his title, and this companionable man introduced us to his son-in-law, Lord David Cecil at Oxford and his friend Joyce Cary. Cecil had written biographies that interested me extremely, and it struck me that English biographies were usually better than American because the interest in character in England was not frittered away by Freudianism. I had not, in 1951, read Joyce Cary, though I was soon to make the acquaintance of *The Horse's Mouth*. MacCarthy said to me, "Have you noticed that the good writers are often bad men, and that the good men are often bad writers?"—a variation of the French phrase *Bel esprit mauvais caractère* that I had indeed noticed but rather late in life. For I was so incurably romantic about writers that I wished to think of them as good in all respects,—like the pearl-oysters, the rare creatures in whom the precious deposit exists,—and Robert Frost had said to me once, "You want to believe that great writers are good men. It's an illusion that dies hard." Had I derived the illusion from Ruskin, who thought that artists had to be good until he discovered that they had to be "a little wicked?" Or was it a survival in me of the classic notion of Longinus that "great writing is the echo of a great soul?" I am sure that Paul Rosenfeld had felt as I did, and I have known several artists who seemed to me angelic,—while Maxwell Perkins, who had an extensive knowledge of contemporary writers, said, "They are all sons of bitches." I had found in time that writers were, as often as not, jealous and mean, egotistical, petty and even bad-hearted, "lovers of humanity, by the book," as Dostoievsky put it, although I had also noticed that those who associate with the poor think better of human nature than those who associate with the rich. For me, Dr. Jung had said, in *Modern Man in Search of a Soul*, the last word on this subject: "The artist's life cannot be otherwise than full of conflicts, for two forces are at war within him—on the one hand, the common human longing for happiness, satisfaction and security in life, and on the other a ruthless passion for creation which may go so far as to override every personal desire. The creative forces can drain the human impulses to such a degree that the personal ego must develop all sorts of bad qualities— ruthlessness, selfishness and vanity—and even every kind of vice, in order to maintain the spark of life and to keep itself from being wholly bereft."

While in England, we met Chiang Yee, who had lived there for many years and who was to become in the future a very dear friend, the "Silent Traveller" for whose book on New York I had written a brief admiring preface. Chiang Yee, the painter and writer, born in Kiu-Kiang on the Yangtse river, had been the district governor and a magistrate there, but, unsympathetic with the Chinese political world, he had settled in the West in 1933. In *A Chinese Childhood*, he had related the story of the family house in which fifty persons had lived, including a few servants; and he had followed in the footsteps of his father, a painter of birds, butterflies and flowers, to which the Chinese as a race were devoted. He and his friends on walking trips had sketched and improvised poems at picturesque and legendary spots in the mountains, especially Lu mountain near Kiu-Kiang where the poet Li Po had sung and painted. The "Silent Traveller," the title he adopted, was a translation of his Chinese pen-name, which might have been literally rendered as Dumb Walking Man. His work as a civil servant had kept him talking day and night, and, glad enough to escape from this, he had chosen a name that was not unlike the common phrase for a roaming Buddhist monk.

Living in England, Chiang Yee had come to know the quiet things in the countryside, birds, flowers, trees and streams, and he wrote to me, "It is my strong belief that every creature under heaven desires a kind of simple peaceful life." The English lake district, the subject of one of his books, was a happy field for a Chinese artist, and, while he wrote about this region with a singular freshness and lightness of touch, he interpreted it also in idiograms and pictures. Unaccustomed, as he said, to occidental media and technique, he used his Chinese brushes, inks and colours, following his own native method in painting, and in this and his subsequent travel-books, dealing with English and Scottish themes, he produced effects that were equally novel and charming. He was especially fortunate perhaps because England is a land of mists and fogs, like those one saw in so many of the great Chinese paintings, and the fickle English weather pleased him by constantly changing the aspects of scenes while it stirred him to record the changes in his own feelings. With a veil of rain familiar objects passed through enchanting variations, and even his affection for sunshine increased because it arrived unexpectedly and because, like the objects themselves, it was elusive. He delighted in the soft fresh English green that had, as he remarked, both life in itself and the power of blending other colours, and at every turn the simple things of this countryside that was foreign to him carried his imagination back to China. A group of oaks with twisted trunks or a waterfall on a rugged cliff recalled to his mind's eye some old Sung painting, so that sometimes he followed the Sung style in a picture of his own, and, remembering the poets, hermits and scholars who had meditated on scenes like these, he was prompted to repeat their sayings and anecdotes about them. He was charmed by a cluster of horses in a meadow, by a heathery hillock, green and blue, fading into grey, melting into the dove-coloured sky, by dragonflies clinging to the tops of reeds, a knot of water-lily leaves and buds, a robin or a rose-tree in full bloom. Composing a poem now and then, he interspersed his observations with delightful examples of Chinese calligraphy also, with notes on characters whom he had met, wayfaring folk in city streets, old buildings and the customs of the country. Chiang Yee shared Wordsworth's pleasure in the meanest flower that blows. With none of the clichés of travel-writing, his books possessed the companionable charm of a mind of great natural distinction that was willing to be pleased.

In Oxford, Chiang Yee took us to call on Professor Gilbert Murray, who kept open house on Sunday afternoons, at the villa on Boar's Hill where I was touched by a sign at the gate, "Please come in and look at the flowers." An Italian boy, a student from Rome, a nephew of Lauro de Bosis, and a German girl were there that day, and I liked the remark of Lady Mary Murray, "If you don't believe in progress, out of the house you go!" To the grand old scholar, Gilbert Murray, stoicism was a good system of conduct for those who do not accept revelation but still keep some faith in the purpose of things, and, ninety or more at this time, he was broadcasting still in London, a fine Australian Irishman who was a champion of the under-dog. For he knew as well as Aristotle that a man cannot live a complete life when he is miserably poor or deprived of freedom. Sixty-seven years before, he had been married at Castle Howard, to which we had also been taken by my Roman Catholic connections. They lived near Carlisle, and there, at Great Corby, my stepsister's nephew, Monsignor Christopher Lamb, took us to see the ancient Roman wall.

When we returned to America, we found Chiang Yee again, and, in fact, he soon came to live there. I had wondered if he would find New York congenial. With his fondness for grey rainy days and the misty-moisty English scene, would he like the hard dry light of our stone and steel? In New York he would have for mountain peaks only metallic skyscrapers, and instead of the soft English rain he would have our thoroughly business-like rain that comes down as if it were also made of steel. But he soon found cherry-trees in blossom, in the parks and botanical gardens, and willows with branches tossing in the wind that stirred him to write poems as he painted and drew them, and even the natural rock-formations, the water-falls, thickets and gorges that were immemorial subjects of Chinese painters. There were squirrels with sparkling eyes that were also cherished in Chinese art, and almost every one of his pictures contained a pigeon, a swan, a crane, or wild geese, ducks or sea-gulls flying aloft. He found ponds with white lotus in full bloom, and tall buildings that looked like bamboo shoots as they emerged from the tops of low-hung clouds. In the Yosemite, with a Chinese friend, he wandered around Mirror Lake, Chen playing the Chinese bamboo flute and Yee reading aloud some Chinese poems, while the frogs sang with them in the moonlight. The surrounding peaks and cliffs in mist and rain reminded him of his beloved Lu mountain. Chiang Yee repeated the saying of Mencius that a man should retain his childlike mind, a rebuke to our tiresome ideal of "sophistication," and he said that, in securing the freedoms from ignorance and want, we should also plan for a "freedom from too many desires." That was his reply to our foolish cult of advertising, which exists for the breeding of desires, the more the better.

We found our neighbour Lewis Mumford living in monastic simplicity still, planting his onions and beans in spring and alternating his bouts of work with equally quiescent relaxations. Immensely productive, he took time off gardening, reading and sleeping, without a serious thought in his head, keeping this up until he was bored when he supposed that he was cured as well. Loving Tolstoy's sanity and health, he found that Dostoievsky wore now better than Tolstoy because what had once seemed wicked fantasy had become part of our normal and daily existence. For the morals of the rattlesnake were everywhere, and he had a persistent sense that everything was going wrong, that the captain was drunk and the mates were mad and the crew was affected with sleeping sickness. I am quoting from Lewis's letters to me: he said, for instance, that the young had a deep nostalgia for the twenties whose sense of disillusionment, as compared with their own, was one vast iridescent soap-bubble of hope. I wondered why Lewis, who was so well known in England, Sweden, Holland and Poland, was still not properly known in his own country, perhaps because he was a "generalist," not fabricating the pieces but putting them together in a significant picture. Or was it due to the feeling of boredom the older generation produces when people feel they have been around too long? He stood for the restoration and renewal of man, that poor bewildered creature who had become an impoverished exile from the native land he had left and from a world of mechanism that refused to recognize his existence.

Of Helen Keller, whose mind was always focussed on the great impersonal things and who never thought of personal inconsequences, we had seen more and more, and we knew, and could say, that she was exactly what the general public believed she was. Before she went, with Polly, to Japan, she dined with us and the John Sloans, and Helen, who placed her hand on John Sloan's head, exclaimed that it was a "noble head and strong." While she was on her way to Japan, her house at Westport was burned down, with all her manuscripts and letters, her furniture and books, but presently a carload of presents arrived from her friends in Japan, and the new house became a Japanese museum. There were tables, vases, rugs, pictures, carvings, hangings and porcelain, some ancient and the rest made in Hiroshima, a few years after its destruction. Then she wrote from Latin America, "I caught tantalizing glimpses of the mighty Andes, pre-Christian civilizations and varied strains in the populations. Amazing how they have survived after innumerable civil wars,—Aztecs, Incas and other Indian peoples, Portuguese and Spaniards,—with the land problems and the long droughts that aggravate them and the manifold difficulties of farming." She wrote to me from New Zealand, "the beautiful great little country-island." At eighty, she was still writing appeals for the blind, without any touch of vanity herself, rather like an eager child, and always conscious of "America's exasperating faults." We were just emerging, she said, "from a pygmy chauvinism." I gave her Nehru's *Glimpses of World History* to be put into braille for her voracious fingers.

I am sure that Helen Keller would have said with Edmund Wilson, "I believe in human evolution. I don't see how it is possible to reject the evidence that contemporary humanity, with all its faults, has developed from beings much lower, or to fail to draw the conclusion that we are to develop into something higher still. I believe in progress as the eighteenth century people did." She would not have repudiated the French Revolu-

tion that made citizens out of serfs and peasants not long after
Prince Charolais shot tilers on the roofs in Paris for the fun
of seeing them tumble into the street. That was the value of
ordinary men before the age of revolutions, as it had been when
Peter the Great, discovering a new kind of gallows, ordered one
of his servants to be hanged at once so that he could see how
it worked. There had been a time when wars were started over
a cardinal's lapdog and illegitimate babies in Venice were thrown
into the canals before "conservatories" were invented to save
them, a time when prisoners of war were roasted in baker's
ovens and workers were forbidden to establish a pension fund
for their aged members. This was the kind of fact that various
historians refrained from mentioning, those who were anxious
to undo the revolutions, facts that show how "we have become,"
as Bertrand Russell says, "in certain respects progressively less
like animals." Inhumanities of this kind were taken for granted,
unlike Dachau and Buchenwald, which every human being
knows were wrong; and, improvements in these matters were
the result, as Julien Benda said, of the teaching of the eighteenth century, "against which the 'masters of modern thought'
are in complete revolt . . . those who would blush to be able
to say, like Voltaire, 'I have done a little good, 'tis my best
work.'" Even the reactionary Chateaubriand came to accept
the idea of progress, saying that, if society seems sometimes to
move backward, it is always really moving forward. Yet Baude-
laire could say, "Belief in progress is a lazy man's creed, a creed
for Belgians."

Once we visited Edmund Wilson, whom I had known for
three or four decades, in his old family house at Talcottville,
where he underwent, in the phrase of Howells, "the lapse from
the personal to the ancestral which we all undergo in the
process of the years." It was a charming stone house of the early

nineteenth century to which he retreated from Wellfleet when he felt too crowded in summer there; and on the first evening we all went for a picnic on the Independence river in a gully bordered by evergreen trees and damp lichen-covered rocks. This was one of those "up-state" rivers that Rita was homesick for, in Wilson's novel, *I Thought of Daisy*, about which indeed she had written a poem with an image of a "lovely flock of stones" that "tumbled and crashed into splinters the black-silver mirror" of the water below. Evidently, Wilson, like Rita, enjoyed thinking of "the beauty of stony rivers." The Wilsons took us to lunch at the Oneida Community where old Mr. Pierrepont Noyes was still living, the son of the founder in the eugenic free-love days. Wilson had warned us that at first the region would seem rather empty, but that everything filled in around him so that it became more real than Wellfleet; and, in fact, he had been surprised to find that he was surrounded there by the Iroquois national movement of which he was to write. This movement was not unlike Scottish nationalism or Zionism, with a revival of the old religion and claims for the property that had been lost because of the encroaching St. Lawrence seaway. Wilson had been interested earlier in the Zuni Indians of Arizona, one of the multifarious concerns of a critic who could be called, almost uniquely, a writer. He was, for the rest, an eager player of anagrams and other games, along with Chinese chequers.

A highly unreasonable rationalist, abounding in violent prejudices, Wilson had no use for Somerset Maugham, and Aldous Huxley, for him, was not an artist. I could scarcely understand why he disliked the English, with their "British impudence," for example, and this became no clearer to me when he told me that one of his forbears had been shut up in the Revolution in a British prison-ship. Nor could he abide the "dreadful" New

England novels of Howells that Christian Gauss, his Princeton professor, had disliked before him. I had no doubt that Christian Gauss shared with Francis Parkman a misconception of the "rise" of Silas Lapham. But I always thought, nevertheless, of Wilson as the most intelligent writer in the country, one who, in a day of grammarians, led the uncloistered life of a many-sided free-ranging man of letters and the world; for his fount of ideas and images seemed never to falter, his range of interests was so wide and his talents so diverse, he was so universally curious and so generally responsive. An artist in several forms, he had touched as a critic on politics, economics, the theatre and music, on actors, magicians and the so-called lively arts, while he was as much at home with Sophocles and Persius as he was with E. E. Cummings and Thornton Wilder. In *Axel's Castle* he had introduced to a whole generation of readers the masters of the post-war literary epoch, and he was perhaps the most lastingly interesting of the prose celebrants of Greenwich Village in the decade he recalled in plays and essays. He produced in *To the Finland Station* a memorable history of modern revolutionary thought, and he created in *The Little Blue Light* a play that would be classical if our theatre were comparable to the theatre of Strindberg or Ibsen. In the day of Whitman's "orbic" mind, he had studied conversational Greek in Greece, Russian in Russia,—he translated Pushkin,—and later, attracted to Israel, he set to work at Hebrew for a fresh understanding of the Bible and the new republic. He had an incomparable feeling for the literary climate in which he lived, for the changes in the time-spirit from decade to decade, an exciting sensitivity that struck me at almost every point in his panoramic portrait of twentieth-century letters.

With his flexible independent mind, detached from all factions and groups, Wilson seemed to collaborate with a cultivated public; and what could do more to maintain this, to create it and sustain it? Besides, he saw literature in terms not of itself alone but of the life of humanity and its chief interests; and he combined the aesthetic with the psychological, social and historical sense, knowing that one must "see the writer as a man in order to appreciate him as an artist." Personally resembling Sainte-Beuve, learned without being bookish, he possessed supremely the gift of wonder, and his sympathies, like Sainte-Beuve's, were largely with the humanitarians, although he too was a sceptic towards every form of faith. It is true that also, like Sainte-Beuve, his intelligence seemed to look down on his heart, which lay there "like a cold moon"; nor did he seem to have a centre. He was afloat, his ship had no anchor. But what a pleasure it was to read his *causeries,* so nimble in style, with the tone of conversation, and to hear him say, "It is up to American writers to try to make some sense of their American world, for their world is now everybody's world"; and "The thing that's upsetting now in politics and literature both is that from the moment we lose the idea that we are concentrating on this country,—and that idea seems completely to have gone by the board,—we don't know where we are any more." I liked this, as I liked the saying of Katherine Anne Porter in one of the essays of *The Days Before:* "Americans are not going anywhere, and I am glad of it . . . In the present [of the second world war] they must live here or nowhere, and they must share the responsibility of helping to make this a place where men can live as men and not as victims, pawns, a lower order of animals driven out to die beside the road or to survive in stealth and cunning."

CHAPTER XIV

AT SEVENTY-FIVE

I AM WRITING this in Bridgewater, the cross-roads Connecticut
village where we have been living for the last twelve years.
In my study at the front of the house, facing the usually silent
street, are gathered relics of my past, the bronze dog that used
to stand on my grandmother's onyx clock and a cluster of oddly
designed clay pipes from various towns in Europe. My brother
and I as little boys collected these when we were abroad to
bring them to our father who had remained at home. On the
mantelpiece is the red sandstone copy of Hadrian's column
found by my father in Rome once, and, beside that, a re-
production of the death-mask of Randolph Bourne that was
given me by the sculptor long ago. There is the glass bell with
a picture in coloured sand that my other grandmother brought
back from the Isle of Wight and a lithograph portrait of John
Quincy Adams from my great-grandfather's Plattsburg house
that I used to have with me in college. All these trifles that
would never fit into a modern house, and that will be scattered
after my death, seem to me to hold my identity together in the
various chances and changes of life.

As I had grown older, I had felt more and more the truth of
one of Sainte-Beuve's observations. Referring to the river of

literature, which flowed on, wide and deep, he spoke of his own relation to it. "When we are young," he said, "we can run beside it and even get in advance of its course; in middle age we are unable to run ahead of it but can only follow panting beside; and in the end it flows past us and to our astonishment we observe that its surface is black with strange little boats which, even as we look, sail beyond the range of our vision." How many generations of critics had felt as Sainte-Beuve felt! —and I thought of Edmund Wilson, ten years younger than myself, who said he had given up trying to read the books of the new writers. He could not follow the strange little boats that swarmed in the river of literature, although he was full of interest in the world about him. I myself turned away to the past uneasily, keeping an always baffled eye on the writers of the present whom, very often, I could scarcely understand. Or, rather, on the books rather than the writers. Although good novels still appeared, there had ceased to be novelists in the sense of the writers of the nineteen-twenties, and I was struck by the remark of a physician that all the doctors were good now but that the great doctors had ceased to exist. The novels, good and bad, seemed to be sporadic; they did not announce new personalities. Or at least they did not seem to me to do so.

I had preferred to be called an essayist rather than a critic, but I had written criticism, and it seemed to me that all American criticism was impermanent, that none of our generalizations lasted more than a few years. I remembered the famous remark of Stieglitz that every five years we had in this country a new generation. Everything changed from decade to decade and all one wrote became, in a short time, irrelevant and obsolete. An architect whom I once met who had done fine building in New York told me that of the hundred and fifty houses he had put up a hundred and forty-eight had been torn down.

He had not the heart to go on and retired at sixty. It seemed to me that my chief hope for some kind of relative permanence was in my historical series *Makers and Finders*, already out of fashion, from the critical point of view of the present, but, as I felt, certain to come back. Reading for this, and writing it, I had spent a ten or twelve-hour day, virtually every day, for nineteen years. I had read about five thousand books in connection with it. For all the attacks of the critics, I was encouraged by letters that I received from often unknown writers. One of them said, "I feel less a nomad whenever I finish one of your books. Even at my loneliest, I feel sustained by the record of men before me who struggled toward consciousness." Another said that, although it was not orthodox literary history, my series "gave our creative writers for the first time a feeling that there is an American literary tradition to which they belong"; a young novelist wrote to me, "My work grows out of what went before. I feel I'm in the line," and still another said, "One gains a real feeling of participation . . . Our struggles of today fall into a new perspective." That had been my hope and intention, my object being emotional, to awaken feeling and imagination, somewhat in the manner of Standish O'Grady's history of Ireland's heroic age that had such an effect on the Irish revival. But although my history was fully translated into Japanese, and many other languages as well, I was referred to at home with a vague respect in critical circles only as the author of *America's-Coming-of-Age*. Everything I had written since, except *The Ordeal of Mark Twain*, was, as I gathered, best not mentioned. Even in Japan, *America's-Coming-of-Age* was printed, with Japanese notes, as a school textbook.

I remembered the saying of my old editor, Albert Jay Nock, "A nation is a spiritual principle evoked by the common possession of a rich legacy of remembrances," but he added, "A spiritual heritage is about the last thing that our enlightened age could be induced to take stock in." He further said that one's attitude towards one's illustrious dead "marks the difference between a nation and an agglomeration." Knowing that our nation was scarcely formed as yet, I had hoped to contribute towards the forming of it, and seeing that my historical series required an explanation, I then turned to *The Writer in America*. I found I had to defend a philosophy that was implicit in my theme and would have been so taken a few years before, but it was now attacked by the reigning school of critics, a school avowedly intolerant and increasingly dictatorial. Under professions of the Christian religion, this school felt it was entitled, as Lionel Trilling put it, to say "Thou fool" to those who still dared to be independent of it, by no means the first time in history in which religion had proved to be useful in a quest for power. In a period of conformity, with no place for the otherwise-minded,—a period of group-thinkers and hidden persuaders, in which only the adjustable and adaptable were admired,—these critics denied the first principle of all creative endeavour; for, as Darwin said, in *The Origin of Species*, isolation was the chief cause of the appearance of new forms and original creation. And who was to be apart and alone, who was to be isolated, if one accepted the orthodoxy of the fashionable critics?

I composed three biographies, the first one of John Sloan, my old friend of the days of Petitpas, when I dined in his studio with J. B. Yeats and with Rockwell Kent and Robert Henri. In the decades between, I had seen Sloan, off and on, though he went for half the year to Santa Fe, preferring the rocky and sandy landscape there to the summer green world of the East. Then, coming one day to Bridgewater, when we had first settled there, he said he had never seen before the rolling hills of

Connecticut and the great civilized trees in the village streets. He felt like a desert scorpion dropped into a green salad, and, reconciled that day to summers in New England, he presently went to stay in Hanover, New Hampshire. He died a few months later there and his wife Helen turned over to me a mass of John Sloan's papers, carefully arranged, his picturesque diary and assorted letters, so that I was soon able to write the story of this modern Hogarth of New York. Berenson, to whom I sent it, as I sent all my later books, said it was "the most interesting and most delightful story of a modern painter and his achievement that has reached my eyes." But Berenson was not convinced that Sloan had found his way to the calling he was made for, writing about art: "I for instance have scarcely ever encountered in print utterances about painting in particular and art in general so closely parallel to my own, and generally better expressed. Your quotations for his classes enthralled me."

From that time on, Berenson read all my books and sent me the most appreciative remarks about them, one, in particular, *Scenes and Portraits*, about which he said, "How much of it could enter into my own autobiography!" For half the names were of people he had known or known about, "as, e.g., in the cases of Sheldon and Perkins." He read *Days of the Phoenix* "with excitement, zest and the keenest interest," he said of *From a Writer's Notebook* that it had "intellectual breadth and depth always," and in *The Dream of Arcadia* he observed that he was "deeply happy" over the chapter about himself. That book was a return to the feeling of enchantment I had experienced in Italy as a boy. Berenson seemed to like my hagiology of Helen Keller, which I had gone to Los Angeles to write, and he asked me to send him some pictures of the architecture I had found so fresh and engaging there. But to him the houses on Sunset Boulevard looked more like "bird-cages for anthropomorphic bipeds than human habitations." He did not live long enough to read the life of Howells that I had intended to write many years before, a novelist, seldom read any longer, although he was soon to be revived, a symbol of a rejected American past. The critics could see nothing good in Howells's few fine novels that were undoubtedly the best of their time and they continued to parrot his phrase about "the more smiling aspects of life" that was so fully contradicted by his later books. Howells had been far less prudish than Mark Twain, as Bernard De Voto showed after reading manuscripts that most of us had never seen. He was rejected as Sinclair Lewis had been also, the novelist who, in his turn, had rejected Howells. Lewis had called Howells, in his Nobel Prize speech, "a pious old maid whose greatest delight is to have tea at the vicarage," an absurd statement that led me to wonder if Lewis had read the novelist he so made light of. This doubt was confirmed when I lunched with Lewis in New York one day and he asked me to go to a second-hand book-store with him. It was in Fifty-ninth Street, and Lewis asked the bookseller for all the Howells novels he had and carried away at least a dozen volumes. This was years after he had received the Nobel Prize and Lewis said he had never read any of them. I hope they included *The Shadow of a Dream* and *The Son of Royal Langbrith,* which would have put an end to all prejudgements.

Sinclair Lewis, a most lovable man, too impetuous, swift to forgive, and capable of a generous indignation, had given Bernard De Voto the literary trouncing of his life and nominated him for the Institute ten minutes later; and when Hemingway foully attacked him, in *Across the River and Into the Trees,* ridiculing this "pock-marked jerk" for his "craters of the moon face,"—referring to Lewis's facial cancer,—I remembered how, in his speech at Stockholm, Lewis had praised Hemingway and the other novelists of Hemingway's generation. He had worked over his documentation as Hemingway worked over his style, and when he died the critics, ignoring Lewis's vision of life, his broad panorama of America and his passion for justice, condemned him as Hemingway condemned him. Admitting only his earliest novels, they overlooked his development, his hatred of the intolerant, the ignorant, the smug, though he seemed to me more mature than those who discarded him as one discards an old pair of shoes. In *Arrowsmith*, the doctor had won happiness by the exercise of his "will power," unlike the characters of Hemingway who had no will whatever, or who could do nothing against circumstances, and yet, as John Peale Bishop said, "dictated the emotions to contemporary youth."

When Lewis asked in a preface whether "this American optimism, this hope and courage, so submerged now in 1935, are not authentic parts of American life," I remembered how little I had once agreed with Lewis that they are in fact "good things to have." This optimism was nothing to boast of, it sprang from a natural buoyancy, the buoyancy for which Bertrand Russell had once admired America, but it indicated a cult of life as marked as the cult of death that had been so commended in the Spaniards. I remembered again how Gandhi's refusal to concentrate on the bad in people "sometimes added inches or cubits to the height of his associates and even the casual visitor felt its potential benefits." So Louis Fischer commented on Gandhi's "creative optimism." With us, it had certainly survived

> The collapsed structure of moral Europe,
> Of whatever was fought for on either side
> After the Sarajevo pistol shot.

It seemed more than ever to me that the fatalism of our literary circles,—the belief in total depravity, the obsession of evil, and all the old fixed ideas of Calvinism, which had paralyzed the mind of New England before Emerson appeared,—had sprung from the general failure of Europe as a result of the world wars and that our literary mind was too weak to resist it. That is to say, it was still not yet mature enough to withstand the mood of discouragement that prevailed in literary Europe, the "fatigued disillusionment of the fifties," as Spender called it.

For it was certain that our literary mind did not express the country, which still believed, on the whole, in human decency and, as Crane Brinton said, "in some kind of progress . . . we are still heirs of the Enlightenment," he said further; and Paul Tillich, in *The Courage To Be,* spoke of the present-day American courage as "one of the great types of courage to be as a part." For "its self-affirmation is the affirmation of oneself as a participant in the creative development of mankind. . . . There is something astonishing in the American courage for an observer who comes from Europe" and who finds it still present in the large majority of people. For the rest, I could not understand Reinhold Niebuhr's argument that the pursuit of happiness is based on an illusion, happiness being a by-product of harmony and the only reality of life being an endless contest between joy and grief. For what better thing than harmony could one pursue, as the Greeks with such great consequences pursued it? It seemed to me that the thought of Confucius, whom Thomas Jefferson so admired and who believed in the goodness of the natural man, was more tenable than the grim Niebuhrian view of life. Moreover, it explained why American culture, in the phrase of Auden, was still "committed to the future." Americans could never accept the belief of Kierkegaard that "earthly happiness is a sin." They were closer to the Chinese who, as Chiang Yee said, looked upon happiness as the greatest good.

Was not the idea of original sin, so totally unscientific, a parochial European mediæval doctrine, as little shared by the Chinese or the Hindus or the Jews as it had been by our own Emerson and Whitman? Seeing sin and evil everywhere seemed to create more evil and sin, wishing evil on human-kind, impelling it towards evil. And how Whitman would have rejoiced in the thought of contemporary Africa and Asia, in the nations that had escaped from the hollow of the wave, in the displacement of planetary forces that wrecked the European empires and placed these colonial countries in their own pos-session. The despair of Europe was surely the result of its ex-haustion and shrinkage, and generations would have to pass before, in Robert Frost's phrase, it could learn "what to make of a diminished thing." But Europe's extremity had been the opportunity of Asia and Africa, and a limitless horizon opened out before the peoples there, the hope of peaceful activity in free countries. How could Americans feel that the "decline of the West," certainly true for Europe, was true for them? And yet our literary life was still under the European spell and re-flected its apprehension of the end of all things. It disregarded the real feeling of the country, which Faulkner expressed in his speech at Stockholm, "I decline to accept the end of man"; and it took no account of Melville's remark that the time had come for America to "set," not "follow," precedents.

It seemed to me that the time for this had really come. I felt that Americans should set precedents in alliance with Asiatic minds that shared the American buoyancy and vitality; and I agreed with William Carlos Williams, who said about his countrymen, "The Orient, which they fear, is their oppor-tunity to embrace the 'new.'" Helen Keller, journeying round the world, fully understood the aspirations of the Arabs, the Jews, the Japanese, and she carried with her the planetary visions of Emerson and Whitman whom so many Asians took for the American prophets. Then one day Henry Wallace came to see me, glad to be out of politics and certain for another thing that men were never made for travel in space. We spoke of AE, who had told me once that he had come to America mainly to see Wallace, and, talking about Jo Davidson, I put into his hand Jo's old ivory-handled walking-stick, which his wife had brought to me from France. In a speech that Wallace made in our village, he spoke of the need of somehow meeting the mind of the Russians, sure as he also was that Russian communism was bound to fail because it thought only of things and not of life. He took as his motto Walt Whitman's line, "Urge, urge, urge, the procreant urge of the earth." Walt Whitman was always uppermost in the minds of Jo Davidson, of Helen Keller and of Henry Wallace. How did it happen that our writers lagged behind, failing to give us a literature "fit to cope with our occasions," that in their private world they were generally cut off from the great public interests of the time?

Henry Wallace believed that the balance of terror would prevent a third world war. But the thought of the bomb, like the gorgon's eye, turned many minds I knew to stone. Because of it they could not contemplate the future, and it was true that the future lay under the shadow of swords, that everything hopeful in the world at present was a gamble. For this reason the breath of the Western world seemed to have stopped, as if it were in a state of suspended animation, and a young man in San Francisco expressed in a letter to me the spiritual desolation of the sensitive young. "There aren't many of us," he wrote, "who care a particular damn, a few congenital misfits, inveterate malcontents brooding in the public libraries. There are a few of us, serious and sceptical, rather wary, I think, but intensely curious, who wonder what have all the anguished and indignant voices descried and why are they silent. We ask and no one answers. It is as though angry, bold, intemperate words had never been spoken or if, indeed, they had been, they had best be disremembered." In the silence, one could almost have heard a feather drop, as if everyone was waiting for the bomb to fall. We were living in a season closely resembling the decades that preceded the year 1000 when Christians really expected the end of the world.

Then another letter came from a friend in Chicago, "One's only uneasiness is that this is one of those splendid summers, like '14 and '39, when something awful can happen before it ends. But we mustn't think along these lines." Or one had to think with two minds, one of them doing its best to meet the appalling question of missile warfare, and the other harbouring the words *as if*, as if the question of the bomb had been provisionally settled. Emerson quoted Hafiz who described the phrase on the gate of Heaven, "Woe unto him who suffers himself to be betrayed by Fate," and he said, "Men have the power to look not at Fate but the other way. The practical view is the other." In every acre of a quiet lawn, on the loveliest June afternoon, unstylized bull-fights on a miniature scale take place every second. If one's eye were a magnifying-glass one would faint with horror over the stealthy carnage of the worms and insects. The hawk that skims gracefully over the marsh has only murder in its mind and an owl's family requires, for its diet, seven hundred creatures every day, and among these one hundred and fifty mice. Nature is red in tooth and claw, and of course it has to be, but we should lose our wits if we thought about it. Hamilton Basso, who had visited Finland, told me of a case of the practical view. Within a mile from the Russian border he watched a man building a barn, slowly hammering the walls and the beams together, in full sight of the barbed wire and the Russian guns, as if another war were not to be thought of. This man was confiding in the future as if nothing had happened in two world wars to abate the nonchalance with which he regarded it, and why should we not trust the future in the spirit of the Enlightenment the principles of which are not played out, as so many think nowadays? I agreed with Albert Schweitzer that "all real progress in the world is in the last analysis produced by rationalism," and "It will soon become evident that we shall be obliged to take up the same position which the eighteenth century defended so stoutly." Moreover, I agreed with Breasted, the Egyptologist, that what we need more than anything else is confidence in man, and that the story of his rise is a basis for full confidence. The liberal experiment, barely two hundred years old, is of course still immature, but can it be abandoned so lightly?

As for this country, it seemed to me that Alfonso Reyes, the Mexican sage, was right in his essay, *The Position of America:* "Our America should live as though it were always making ready to realize the dream to which its discovery gave rise among the thinkers of Europe, the dream of Utopia, of the happy republic, which lent particular warmth to the pages of Montaigne as he reflected on the surprises and marvels of the New World." We should certainly work for Utopia even if, when we get there, we are bored by its insipidity. It will be time then to imagine something else. Perhaps, long before that, another Buddha may appear and say, "Here are trees,—let us think the matter out"; and mankind will turn its back on offices, factories and motor-cars and set forth on some new kind of adventure.